Leading Dynamic Seminars

Leading Dynamic Seminars

A Practical Handbook for University Educators

James H. Anderson
and
Andrew H. Bellenkes

First published 2013 by
PALGRAVE MACMILLAN

Palgrave Macmillan in the UK is an imprint of Macmillan Publishers Limited,
registered in England, company number 785998, of Houndmills, Basingstoke,
Hampshire RG21 6XS.

Palgrave Macmillan in the US is a division of St Martin's Press LLC,
175 Fifth Avenue, New York, NY 10010.

Palgrave Macmillan is the global academic imprint of the above companies
and has companies and representatives throughout the world.

Palgrave® and Macmillan® are registered trademarks in the United States,
the United Kingdom, Europe and other countries

ISBN 978–1–137–27683–4

This book is printed on paper suitable for recycling and made from fully
managed and sustained forest sources. Logging, pulping and manufacturing
processes are expected to conform to the environmental regulations of the
country of origin.

A catalogue record for this book is available from the British Library.

A catalog record for this book is available from the Library of Congress.

Printed in China

We dedicate this handbook to our beloved wives, Emily Anderson and Susi Bellenkes. Their unbounded patience and compassion made it possible for us to devote the time and effort necessary to complete this work.

Contents

List of Figures and Tables

▶ Figures

▶ Tables

Acknowledgements

As an undergraduate and graduate student, I was fortunate to learn from a great many talented and dedicated seminar leaders at Amherst College and the Fletcher School of Law and Diplomacy, Tufts University. I owe them a debt of gratitude for inspiring my interest in seminar-leading techniques, and I would identify them all by name if the list were not so lengthy. I would also like to thank my former colleagues at the George C. Marshall European Center for Security Studies in Garmisch, Germany, who broadened my exposure to a rich array of international teaching styles. My colleagues at Marine Corps University offered many kind words of encouragement that helped to make the hard work all the more bearable. The publishing team at Palgrave Macmillan, ably lead by Jennifer Schmidt, Project Editor, provided their expertise and cheerful assistance throughout the entire process. Finally, I am especially grateful to wife Emily, who provided many thoughtful suggestions to improve the text.

JAMES H. ANDERSON

I am very grateful to my colleagues Dr Larry Shattuck and his Human Systems Integration Program team at the Naval Postgraduate School in Monterey, California, from whom I have gained a wealth of invaluable experience in the design and presentation of distance-learning-based seminars. I am also much indebted to my colleagues at the George C. Marshall European Center for Security Studies, and especially to Dr Jack Clark, whose world-class Seminar on Trans-Atlantic Civil Security Program has, for me, been the model for excellence in the conduct of *in situ* inquiry-based seminars. Finally, heartfelt thanks to my beloved Susi, for her unwavering moral and critical support during the creation of this narrative.

ANDREW H. BELLENKES

The views expressed in this book are those of the authors and do not necessarily represent the views of the United States Government, the United States Department of Defense or its components.

Introduction

▶ **Introduction**

Our handbook addresses the dynamics of seminar-based education. By 'seminar', we mean a small group discussion led by an educator in pursuit of learning objectives.[1] The seminar contrasts sharply with lecture-based instruction, wherein a member of the academic staff (faculty) attempts to impart knowledge by transmitting it to the students without any opportunity for extended discussion or dialogue.[2] Lectures can be effective in conveying information to a large audience – either in person or by means of the web – but they are not the focus of this handbook.[3]

Some of us have had the good fortune to encounter educators who, by virtue of their own interest and passion for their subjects, have inspired a similar appetite for a topic in us. Their infectious enthusiasm made us eager to attend their seminars, to participate in them, and to share the experience of learning with others. If you have been the instructor of such a seminar, then you know the exhilaration of having your students attend to your every word, and respond thoughtfully and creatively to your questions. You can take deep satisfaction in knowing that you have helped open their minds to something new, something important, and something lasting. This is the dream of every seminar instructor.

Then, there is the grim reality. Far too often, instructors toil for many long hours to craft together a quality seminar, only to find that their students seem to be uninterested and unresponsive, to the point of even falling asleep. The resulting poor post-seminar critiques often prove demoralizing, draining instructors of any motivation to pursue similar efforts thereafter. Scarred by such experiences, these instructors typically cringe at the prospect of having to create and present future seminars.

The problems leading to such negative experiences for seminar students and instructors often have little to do with the materials presented, or the instructor as an individual; rather, they lie in the manner in which the seminar has been created and presented. This is not to imply that instructors must entertain their students with tricks and diversions; clowns belong in circuses, not in seminar rooms. Instead, the instructor must provide the student with the means to see for him- or herself the importance of the material being presented, and thus stimulate the student to learn even more. This is a tall challenge for today's educators, who face increasingly diverse student populations.

One need not despair, however, for the practical techniques that have been shown to help ensure quality seminars can be learned. This book addresses the most vital elements of seminar-based instruction, from start to finish.

▶ Framework

While this book has a practical orientation, it is based on an educational framework known as 'inquiry-based learning'.[4] As the term suggests, this framework emphasizes the active pursuit of student knowledge and understanding by means of questions and research problems. This approach is student-centric, with the emphasis on student learning and reflection, rather than the delivery of a curriculum, *per se*.

▶ The Socratic Method

The Socratic Method of questioning provides a core foundation for seminar-based instruction and, as such, it is a central driver of inquiry-based learning. While this powerful technique remains essentially unchanged from the time of Socrates, the environment in which today's educators must operate has evolved considerably since antiquity. Thus, we will explain how the Socratic Method can best be adapted to the modern era in order to:

- encourage student contributions to seminar discussion, especially those who would otherwise prefer to remain silent or disengaged
- address sensitive topics with finesse, turning difficult conversations into teachable moments
- transform potentially disruptive students into allies for collaborative learning
- connect with students representing a host of nationalities and cultures, especially those whose native tongue might not be English

- exploit technologies in a thoughtful manner to enhance seminar-based instruction
- assess learning outcomes.

▶ Why this book is needed

Every generation of students presents challenges to educators, and the current generation is no exception. Students today generally have shorter attention spans than their predecessors, especially with respect to learning methods that lack interactivity.[5] This does not mean educators should dumb down their instruction, or even shorten seminar time. But they do need to give careful consideration to how best to engage today's students in pursuit of learning outcomes.

Another salient characteristic of today's students is their affinity for technology. Reliant on technological devices from an early age, many students have become dependent on these technologies for communication, intellectual engagement and stimulation. This presents a challenge to instructors, insofar as the essential techniques for seminar-based instruction are not dependent on technology, though seminars may benefit from its careful and selected application. Seminar instructors must therefore find a balance between the use of technological and non-technological approaches to education, exploiting these resources while reinforcing the need for direct student–instructor and student–student discourse that, ultimately, defines a quality learning environment.

Educators also face a broader array of students and learning styles than ever before. Whether presented in a classroom setting or by means of telecommunications, students attending seminars today come from a host of nations and cultures. This presents special challenges and opportunities, especially when instructors must present seminars to non-native English speaking students, some of whom may be new to the interactive nature of seminar discourse. In addressing these opportunities, the authors will draw on their experiences as seminar leaders who have led hundreds of seminars, both in the United States and abroad, for students from Europe, Eurasia, the Middle East, Africa, and elsewhere around the globe.

▶ Who should read this book

Our book will be helpful to anyone who is called upon to create, provide and lead seminars in an educational setting. Junior faculty members, who may lack practical experience – and, therefore, confidence – in the seminar room, will find this book especially valuable.

While there are exceptions, Western academic institutions seldom provide candidates for advanced academic degrees with formal instruction in how to run a seminar. For the most part, institutions of higher learning assume that junior faculty members will emulate the teaching methods of their more experienced colleagues, employing their techniques and practices. This approach is problematic, however, because these experienced colleagues may have, over many years, perpetuated mediocrity in the seminar room.

The core challenge for conducting an effective seminar is to be able to find that often delicate balance between meeting the needs of both the educator and those to be educated; to discover, through quality discourse and selective applications of modern technologies, the pathway to finding, and subsequently expanding, the students' interests. In the end, the students' intellectual needs are crucial, and seminar instructors must either adapt their teaching techniques and methods to meet these needs, or risk failure. For this reason, even experienced seminar leaders will find the book of value, since they will be introduced to new techniques and best practices with which they may be unfamiliar. For example, they are likely to gain by considering how best to harness the latest advances in technology discussed in our handbook, to include distance learning.

Academic deans and support staff will also find this text useful. To be effective, academic administrators need to know how best to support seminar instructors in the classroom. They may well wish to use this book to encourage new faculty to learn new techniques, and more senior faculty to refresh theirs. For example, the chapters can provide a template for faculty development sessions prior to the beginning of the school year. Academic deans may wish to consider assigning one faculty member to provide a summary of each chapter, focusing on how the techniques discussed can be applied to their specific department.

Audio-visual support staff members also need to know how technology can be tailored to support educational outcomes. They will profit from reading Chapter 7, on using technology in the seminar room.

Finally, for the seminar instructor, this book will assist you in getting to know your students with the aim of leading them on dynamic and enriching seminar experiences. The development and execution of your seminars must be student-centred. Among other things, this means you must understand who your students are – their intellectual strengths and weaknesses, as well as their educational aspirations and goals. Beyond knowing your students, academic excellence requires the constant testing and evaluation of pedagogical techniques. This book is designed to explain and illustrate a wide range of practical techniques linked with inquiry-based learning that have proven effective in the seminar room.

This book is necessary because student passivity and silence in the seminar room are unacceptable. Naturally, student engagement in seminar discussions is a better outcome than silence, but this still falls short of what educators should seek to achieve in their seminars. The ideal to promote is a stimulating environment where thoughtful and creative student contributions foster both individual learning and collaborative learning for the seminar group. This book is designed to help you, the educator, achieve this imperative.

1 The Socratic Method

Time exacts a heavy toll on the physical world. All is finite, transient. Stone crumbles. Iron rusts. Wood rots. Ideas and concepts have life spans as well, but some fall into disuse or disrepute. The most powerful ones, however, can exist for a very long time indeed. The Socratic Method, an enduring legacy of ancient Greece, is one such idea.[1]

The essence of the Socratic Method – the ability to ask questions to further student knowledge and understanding – is a powerful tool for learning. The Socratic Method fits neatly within the framework of inquiry-based learning, which places students at the centre of the learning process as they pursue questions and research problems. The inquiry-based learning approach stands in contrast with more traditional models of education, where educators seek to transmit knowledge to the student, who is assumed to be a passive recipient of knowledge.[2]

The Socratic Method itself is part science and part art. The science derives from using the logic inherent in reasoned discourse; the art derives from both natural abilities and learned behaviour. This handbook presumes that the art and science involved in leading a seminar can be taught.

Of course, improvement along these lines is not always easy or rapid, but it is possible with patience and determination. Were this not the case, then efforts to educate the educators, including this book, would be a waste of time. This chapter will discuss the origins of the Socratic Method, explore why it works, and consider adaptations that are necessary to ensure its continued relevance.

▶ History of the Socratic Method

Socrates (469 BC–399 BC) was an Athenian philosopher who tutored Plato. He developed the idea of using questions and dialogue to uncover the truth. The Socratic Method was used two millennia before modern educators rediscovered the benefits of what is now widely referred to as 'active learning', where instructors engage their students in dialogue instead of simply lecturing to them.[3]

After the decline of the Greek civilization, the Socratic Method remained relatively dormant, except for its use in the tutorial system of teaching at elite British universities – primarily Oxford and Cambridge – which dates back to the Middle Ages. The tutorial approach drew heavily upon the Socratic Method and typically focused on a very small number of students (usually two or three). In the United States, the Socratic Method existed outside the mainstream of secondary education until it was reintroduced into Western universities (very selectively) during the latter half of the twentieth century.[4]

Modern educators have used the Socratic Method to teach a wide variety of subjects, to include the social sciences and the hard sciences as well (Plato's *Meno Dialogue* details how Socrates used his method of questioning to address ethical and geometry problems). In the modern era, this method has found favour in some professional education, especially regarding business and law.[5]

What is the Socratic Method?

The Socratic Method involves the seminar leader's skilful use of question-driven dialogue to deepen their students' understanding of the given subject matter.[6] Informed questioning and student participation lay at the core of this approach. The technique requires students to think for themselves as they attempt to articulate and defend their ideas. The questioning may typically probe core assumptions, as well as the validity of key inferences and conclusions. In so doing, the questioning engages students at a much higher level than occurs with the mere recitation or memorization of facts. The method encourages students to better question their own reasoning, in a deliberate and self-aware way, as they prepare for challenges beyond the seminar room.

Relevance to the modern world

'The changing nature of teaching reflects the changing nature of society itself.'[7]

Educational requirements do not exist in a vacuum. They reflect economic requirements of states, and these have changed in scale considerably since Socrates' time.[8] Increased economic interdependence, often referred to as 'globalization', has created unprecedented challenges and opportunities for states, both large and small.

Financial and economic crises have become more severe, transmitting shocks from country to country and region to region more rapidly and forcefully than ever before, thus placing unprecedented strains on traditional societies. Many governments have become saddled with crippling debt, having spent well beyond their means. Widespread economic and financial dislocation has resulted in a greater number of people changing jobs more frequently than ever before. This trend runs in parallel with a growing demand for managers and leaders who can operate in an increasingly complex and interdependent world. These systemic changes in the work force place a high premium on critical thinking skills which underlie many professions.

Despite pockets of excellence, colleges and universities are not adequately preparing their students for the full range of twenty-first-century challenges. The brute reality is that students who excel and prosper professionally often do so despite their educational experiences, not because of them. Modern economies need graduates who are capable of bringing innovative and creative problem-solving skills to bear on complex problems. And this, in turn, is where the Socratic Method comes into play.

Civility and the Socratic Method

A certain level of civility and decorum is necessary to use this technique. Unfortunately, the civility that the Socratic Method requires for reasoned discourse is at odds with the incivility which all too often characterizes the modern age. For all its positive benefits – and there are many – the internet has also made civil discourse far more challenging. Internet chat rooms and postings often degenerate into name-calling and sloganeering, especially when controversial topics are discussed. Rudeness and vulgarity have become staples of internet-based commentary.

Reasoned discourse is essential not only for civilized society, but also for representative government as well. Democratically elected leaders engage their citizens in a broad, often open-ended dialogue of questions and answers. The intellectual give-and-take represents far more than an academic exercise; it represents the exercise of freedom which underlies the very logic of democracy, regardless of its historical or cultural particulars.[9] A tolerance for opposing viewpoints and respect for the opinions of others are prerequisites for civilized society.

How the Socratic Method differs from other types of learning

To be sure, the Socratic Dialogue is not the only means of student learning. Self-study, faculty student tutorials, peer-to-peer learning and lectures also play a role in education. But the Socratic Dialogue has unique advantages over these and other educational techniques. The Socratic Method engages students in ways that other forms of learning cannot.

The Socratic Method can help create knowledge and spur problem-solving. However, it does not provide a 'quick and easy' shortcut to knowledge, or accommodate impatient teachers or students. The aim of critical thinking is not speed *per se*, but the pursuit of greater understanding and insight.

Socratic Method and Bloom's taxonomy

The Socratic Method is a practical and flexible instrument. Socrates never precisely defines his methodology for asking questions, though he demonstrates its utility, as evident in Plato's dialogues.[10] The Socratic Method provides an intellectual motor for moving discussions forward in a structured way. At one level, the Socratic Method is *destructive*, insofar as persistent questioning can be used to demolish weak arguments and positions. But, at a deeper level, the aim of the Socratic Method is *constructive*, in that it furthers student understanding and learning.[11]

Benjamin Bloom's landmark taxonomy of higher learning provides a useful framework for thinking about inquiry-based learning in general and the Socratic Method in particular.[12] The taxonomy specifies different levels of cognitive processes involved in the process of learning, ranging from rote memorization to more demanding intellectual endeavours.

How Bloom's taxonomy has evolved

Bloom's taxonomy has attracted close scrutiny since its introduction, and it remains a useful framework for modern educators. Numerous educators have sought to refine and amplify the original framework, and some have succeeded in making useful improvements. In Figure 1.1, for example, Overbaugh and Schultz make several edits beyond changing nouns into verbs: substituting 'remembering' for 'knowledge', 'understanding' for 'comprehension', and 'creating' for 'synthesis'.

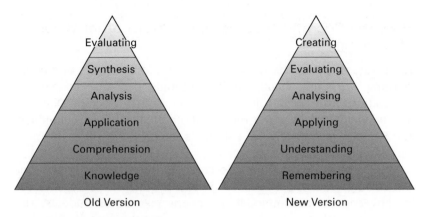

Figure 1.1 Bloom's taxonomy

Source: Overbaugh and Schultz (available at http://ww2.odu.edu/educ/roverbau/
Bloom/blooms_taxonomy.htm; accessed January 2013). Reproduced with the
permission of Richard C. Overbaugh.

The creation of knowledge is a particularly important refinement
in the context of leading seminars. The creative enterprise occurs at
both individual and collaborative levels. This is the hardest level to
achieve, but also the most rewarding. Over time, more ambitious
attempts to revise Bloom's taxonomy have turned his initial pyramid
into ever more elaborate diagrams, including wheels and polygons
that link together categories of cognition, action verbs and learning
outcomes.[13]

That said, neither Bloom's pyramid, nor subsequent modifications
and elaborations thereof, mean much unless the seminar leader is
skilled in using the Socratic Method. Questioning, in a sustained and
thoughtful manner, allows the instructors to bring action verbs –
evaluating, analyzing, synthesizing, and so on – to life in the seminar
room.

Why the Socratic Method works

The Socratic Method works well because it taps into two deeply-
rooted human needs: the quest for knowledge and the desire to
connect with other human beings. Intellectually and socially, the
Socratic Method connects seminar leaders and their students in an
interactive relationship. As such, the Socratic Dialogue thus places
greater intellectual demands on students than do other modes of
education – such as self-study, rote memorization, or listening to

lecturers, however useful they may be at times. The ability to connect students through the Socratic Method provides opportunities for collaborative learning in a structured environment.

The Socratic Method can be used effectively wherever active discourse takes place, since this technique is not dependent on a particular setting. It can be used effectively in a wide variety of venues, ranging from traditional university classrooms to seminars conducted during tours of historic battlefields. The Socratic Method can take place in small classes, as well as in cyberspace. Of course, some venues work better than others, but the Socratic Method has endured into the modern era in part because of its remarkable versatility.

Ultimately, in the seminar setting, the Socratic Method depends on skilled leaders and receptive students. The former is the most important variable. A skilled seminar leader can challenge and inspire unmotivated students to improve their performance. But seminars led by unskilled leaders will flounder, regardless of how motivated the students may be.

The Socratic Method has endured for so long because of its inherent appeal to our social and rational natures. But for reasons that will soon become clear, some adaptations are necessary to ensure its continued relevance and vitality as an educational tool. Whether species survive or become extinct depends on how well they adapt to changing environmental conditions. The logic of adaptation also holds true for educational institutions and the methods they use.

▶ Twenty-first-century students

There is a natural temptation to wax nostalgic about the 'golden days of yesteryear'. But human nature does not change, and the challenges faced by students remain remarkably consistent over time, even allowing for cultural differences.

That said, some differences are worth noting. Clearly, students today are more comfortable using technology than any previous generation; they were, after all, born into a world where technology penetrates every facet of their lives.[14] As a consequence, most expect their instructors will use some type of instructional technology to assist them in the classroom.

Their agility and preoccupation with technology comes with a cost. Students today seem to have shorter attention spans than their predecessors;[15] as a result, they appear much more easily distracted. Students with short attention spans often find it difficult, at least initially, to discern the benefits of the Socratic Method. For this reason, scheduling a two- or three-hour seminar without any breaks is likely to be counterproductive. Seminar instructors should not assume that their students have the interest or ability to engage in a structured dialogue.

Several pedagogical implications follow from this discussion. Students today are more likely to engage in several activities or tasks concurrently (multitask) than their predecessors.[16] Doing so requires them to divide their attention ... to 'timeshare' their limited cognitive resources amongst these various activities which, to some extent, can result in performance decrements associated with one or more of these activities. This presents seminar leaders with yet another challenge, since Socratic Dialogue and multitasking simply do not mix well. The Socratic Method is a focused technique, requiring seminar leaders to promote an environment wherein students are encouraged to attend, engage, participate and, ultimately, contribute to the collaborative learning. The Socratic Method requires a high level of concentration that is at odds with multitasking.

Teaching increasingly diverse student populations

Students are also more diverse than ever before. Immigration patterns are changing the composition of university classrooms worldwide, as students gravitate to universities and programmes that are most capable of promoting critical thinking skills among their students. One striking trend in recent years involves the rising number of international students in Western educational institutions.

As we shall see in Chapter 8, distance learning seminars are bringing together students from around the globe, making irrelevant constraints of time, space, and distance that, prior to the advent of distance learning, dictated whether or not a student would be able to participate in a seminar.

With this in mind, it is important to note that the Socratic Method can – and must – be adapted for groups of culturally diverse students. Sometimes it is necessary to address such issues head on. But cultural differences in the seminar can only enhance discourse; they should never be used as an excuse to avoid using this method. This means, among other things, that instructors need to place the

Socratic Method in a larger context prior to use, lest they risk intimidating students who are unfamiliar with the give-and-take dialogue inherent in the Western tradition.

Diversity is not just a matter of race and ethnicity. Some students are fortunate enough to have a menu of educational options – chief among them education in the home, and parochial, public (state) and private schooling. This means that their receptivity to university-level Socratic discourse will vary depending on their educational background.

Increased diversity among students does not mean that seminar leaders need to 'dumb down' their discourse by lowering its nature, quality or scope. Doing so would clearly prove to be short-sighted and self-defeating since numerous studies have demonstrated how such expectations can be self-fulfilling.[17] The presence of such diversity actually provides seminar leaders with the golden opportunity to raise the intellectual bar by drawing out a broader range of strengths that naturally exists within a diverse student population.

When properly used, the Socratic Method has extraordinary power to link students from wide-ranging backgrounds in a common intellectual dialogue. This capacity to connect at the level of intellectual dialogue is, in fact, a distinguishing feature of what it means to be human. Animals do not engage in Socratic Dialogue, except in cartoons or films.

Teachers must adapt, too

The Socratic Method requires energy and effort on behalf of the student and the instructors. For many instructors, it takes more effort to plan and execute a seminar than it does to prepare and deliver a lecture. The mental, and even physical, strain can be considerable if instructors are unskilled in this technique. There is an element of uncertainty involved, since no one can predict the precise trajectory of discussions guided by this method. This reality can be unsettling for professors who are used to exercising control in the seminar room.

Use of the Socratic Method does not come easily to most academics. As noted in our Preface, only a small number of professors receive any type of formal training in the arts of seminar leading, and the skill sets that make for excellent researchers and writers may not prove to be readily transferable to the seminar room.

Technology

Chapter 7 of this book provides some insights as to how one can effectively incorporate technology into the seminar room. This has been a challenge for a long time, but the accelerating pace of technological change makes this challenge more difficult than ever before. Technology does not render the Socratic Dialogue obsolete. The judicious application of technology can, in fact, enhance the Socratic Method. But technology is a double-edged sword. As we will see, its misapplication can undermine a seminar leader's ability to use the Socratic Method.

▶ Summary

The Socratic Method has endured for 24 centuries, though its use through the centuries has been episodic. Its appeal is deeply rooted in human nature, especially the desire for knowledge and understanding. By emphasizing question-driven discourse, the Socratic Method differs from more passive approaches to learning, such as listening to lectures. As this chapter has stressed, the Socratic Method requires a high level of energy and commitment from educators who engage their students in a sustained dialogue, instead of simply transmitting information in the form of a lecture.

The Socratic approach may appear quite intimidating to students at first, but it can be richly rewarding if applied correctly. If anything, the Socratic Method is more important now than ever before, given the demand for critical thinking skills in the modern economy. Of course, the modern era also presents challenges that Socrates could not even imagine, including an increasingly diverse and tech-savvy student body population, and their preference for instant gratification. But the good news is that these challenges can be overcome with skill, dedication, and patience.

The primary responsibility for adapting the Socratic Method to twenty-first-century realities lies with seminar leaders. The Socratic Method requires judgement in application. Seminar leaders must develop a sense of how far and how fast they can push their students. They need an appreciation for the universality of the technique and specific context in which the technique is applied. As with most educational prescriptions, this is easier said than done. And it is to these efforts that we now turn.

KEY CHAPTER TAKEAWAYS

▶ The promotion of critical thinking skills is the greatest educational imperative for universities and colleges. Inquiry-based learning is a means to this end.

▶ The Socratic Method fits well within the broader framework of inquiry-based learning.

▶ Adapting the Socratic Method to twenty-first-century students requires an appreciation of the method itself and the targeted student population.

2 Prepare your seminar for success

▶ Preparation timeline

- Coordinate with Department Head
- Review departmental objectives
- Formulate course objectives
- Formulate class objectives
- Select readings
- Draft and revise syllabus
- Submit syllabus for approval
- Check room review class roster

Inquiry-based learning does not occur in a vacuum. Numerous studies have documented the importance of creating an environment conducive to learning.[1] Preparation for your seminar involves a wide range of tasks, ranging from the intellectually challenging to the mundane. They are all important, because any shortcoming will weaken the entire course. Problems during the early part of the course are especially troublesome, since they will undermine your credibility if they could have been prevented with a little foresight.

Preparation requires both taking *a priori* action to avoid problems and developing a mindset to promote success well before the seminar actually begins. This chapter will cover both elements in detail.

Advance preparations provide several benefits to you as the instructor. First, they will provide you with an extra dose of confidence at the outset of the course. You will stride into the seminar room on opening day knowing that you have done everything within your power to ensure the success of your seminar. Next, by test driving everything you plan to use in the seminar room, you will have time to uncover potential problems and remedy them before class begins. Also, advance preparations will help you avoid last minute scrambling, which always increases the potential for mistakes and frayed nerves. Finally, your preparations will become clear to your students and set a positive example for them to follow as they prepare to engage and contribute in the seminar room.

There is no magic ratio for the number of preparation hours and the number of execution hours. But the former should always exceed the latter, and typically by a large margin, especially if you are drafting a course from scratch.

▶ Initial preparations

You must be thoroughly familiar with all the course materials. If you have to create the course yourself, then it is assumed that you will already possess this level of familiarity. However, it is always wise to ensure that both your knowledge and course resources are timely and accurate. If you are fortunate, then there may even be a faculty guide that outlines standards, expectations, and procedures for developing courses.

However, if you are 'inheriting' a required course that someone else in the department has already developed, then you may not have the same in-depth background as that of the creator of the course. If this is the case, then you will need to increase your preparation time to become comfortable with all the material. While there is some truth to the axiom that one learns best by teaching, it behoves the course inheritor to have a firm grasp of the materials well before the first day of the seminar.

If available, access student critiques of seminars from previous years. Look for recurring themes, criticisms and complaints, as well as the positive comments in the critiques, and then ask yourself what you can or must do to address them in your course. For example, the recurring problem may be as simple as ensuring that the readings are posted in a timely manner. Or, the problem may be far more difficult – for example, addressing issues such as thematic or conceptual coherence.

As noted, not all the comments in the student critiques will be negative, of course. Take note of the positives; they, too, should inform how you approach leading the seminar. Remember, as your seminar is student-centred, one of your goals here is to reinforce success. If the student critiques indicate a class exercise was especially helpful or a guest lecturer was particularly well-received then, if possible, be sure to retain, or even amplify, these elements in your seminar.

▶ Developing courseware

Course objectives

As indicated in Figure 2.1, there is a hierarchy of educational objectives in every university setting. In most cases, university and department objectives will be beyond your direct control as a seminar leader, though you may have some say in their development, depending on the extent to which university administrators and academic deans seek faculty input. In any event, you need to be familiar with these higher-level objectives to ensure that your course is in alignment with them.

Course objectives are in your domain. They will drive the seminar: its focus, the assigned readings, the exams, the evaluations, and so on. Course objectives should be limited in number; too many objectives could generate confusion. Ideally, there should be three to five course objectives, since this number will help to focus the course.

Equally important, these objectives should seek to engage the students towards the higher levels of Bloom's taxonomy of higher

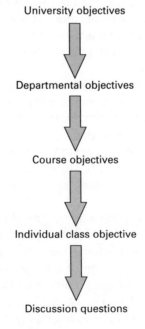

Figure 2.1 Developing courseware

learning. The use of action verbs should specify what the students should be able to do, such as *contrast, evaluate, synthesize,* and *differentiate.*

Example

Students who complete the History of the Italian Renaissance will be able to:

▶ explain how the Italian Renaissance developed and matured
▶ analyze its intellectual and artistic roots
▶ evaluate the lasting impact on the Italian Renaissance.

Course themes

Themes are more general than specific lesson objectives. They help provide your students with some additional insight into what the course will cover. Themes provide the conceptual glue that helps to bind the course together.

Example

Introduction to Psychology will:

▶ highlight the interplay between parental and peer group influences on the development of one's personality
▶ emphasize how the nature-versus-nurture debate impacts personality development
▶ Illustrate how factors that influence personalities are common across cultures.

Course themes are related to course objectives, but the latter specify what students should be able to achieve, whereas the former outline ideas and concepts that recur in varying degrees throughout the course.

Individual lesson objectives

One level below the course objectives are specific lesson objectives for each class. These are more tightly drawn and focused than the course objectives.

Example

Analyze Macbeth's decision to murder the King.

Example

Evaluate Lady Macbeth's relationship to her husband both before and after he murders the King.

Preparing your course syllabus

By 'syllabus' we mean a faculty-generated document that outlines the course objectives, requirements and expectations for the students. The syllabus provides you and your students with a roadmap for the course. As such, you must pay careful attention to its creation, drafting and refinement.

If you create your own syllabus, then at some point you will almost certainly need to have a department head or academic dean review and approve your course syllabus. While the precise timelines will vary from institution to institution, you should seek to secure approval as early as possible. In doing so, you can avoid the scrambling that invariably comes with having to make any last minute changes.

If there are going to be significant changes from the previous year – or if you are teaching a completely new course – then it is strongly advised that you discuss the proposed changes with your departmental supervisor well before you begin drafting the text. Efforts to get the 'buy-in' of your superior should be done in person, if at all possible, and followed up with an email to confirm the substance of the conversation. You may even want to have a trusted colleague review the syllabus at some point. A second set of eyes is often helpful, especially if you are creating your syllabus from scratch.

The syllabus should provide your students with a clear sense of what the course seeks to achieve and how it intends to achieve these objectives. If you fail to articulate this clearly in your syllabus, then it will become that much more difficult for your students to discern your expectations for the seminar.

Checklist for a successful syllabus

- ▶ Does the syllabus provide an introduction that clearly explains the importance of the topic and places it within a larger context?

- ▶ Does the syllabus support the objectives of the department and the institution?

- ▶ Are the course objectives clearly articulated?

- ▶ Are the course requirements (seminar participation, papers, exams, and so on) spelled out?

- ▶ Is the syllabus easy to read (font, boldface headers, and so on) and free of typos?

- ▶ Is your contact information (phone, email address) provided, together with your office hours?

- ▶ Does the syllabus indicate your teaching methodologies for the course?

- ▶ Does the syllabus set high expectations for students insofar as class preparation and participation is involved?

- ▶ Are the required and recommended readings clearly identified?

Course metrics

The critical importance of metrics to evaluate progress will be considered more fully in Chapter 10. However, it should be noted here that developing these metrics is an essential part of your course preparation. The failure to develop metrics – or a slapdash effort to apply them afterwards – is almost certain to end in disaster.

In developing your course and lesson objectives, you must consider how you will measure success. As a general rule of thumb, this becomes easier the more precise you are in formulating your course objectives, as well as your individual class objectives.

Example 1

Understand the nature of modern educational theory.

Example 2

Contrast inquiry-based learning with rote memorization.

Consider the contrast between Examples 1 and 2. The first example is extremely vague and broad. 'Understanding' can take place on many different levels. It may be deep, superficial, or perhaps somewhere in between these two extremes. The second example provides more specific language and requires the student to be able to achieve something that is measurable.

Reading materials

The reading materials provide the intellectual fuel for your seminar discussions. They must support the course objectives, not the other way around.

You must take great care in selecting your readings. If they are too esoteric, they will discourage all but your most ardent students and dampen whatever enthusiasm your students may have for the course. On the other hand, readings that fail to offer sufficient challenge can result in thoroughly bored students.

If your readings must be posted online, then make sure that you check each one well before the course begins to ensure your students will not encounter any problems downloading the material. If there are problems, then contact informational technology support personnel to assist you. Some technological problems are unavoidable for reasons beyond your control (e.g., a university server goes down temporarily), but others are entirely preventable. Your students will forgive for the former, but not the latter. In this regard, be certain also that you are not violating international copyright laws (which vary depending on the national origin of the work) by posting readings online without first obtaining permission. Without such permission, you and your institution/organization could potentially face legal action.

The length and the difficulty of the materials must both be considered when assigning readings. You do not want to confuse your students with a short assignment for one class and a lengthy assignment the following night. Providing a consistent level will help to condition your students to prepare equally well for each of your classes.

If your readings include textbooks, then these should be ordered in plenty of time prior to the start of the seminar, so as to ensure that the texts are available at the first seminar meeting.

Once you have developed your reading assignments, your next

challenge is to ensure that your students do read the assigned materials. Simply encouraging your students with sweet reason will only go so far. Ultimately, the best way to ensure that your students are completing the assignments is to prepare reading-specific questions throughout the course. This approach is especially important to emphasize in the syllabus and during the first couple of seminar meetings.

Asking questions based on the readings will send a clear message to all your students that they are accountable, in a very tangible way, for reading the course material. You may wish to select students at random from the group and ask them to respond. Some may not be able to do so for various reasons, including not having completed the assignment. Others may not be comfortable responding and fail to do so because of nervousness, even if they had read the materials. Do not dwell on these students as doing so may result in embarrassment and negativity about attending the seminar. Encourage them to answer ... even proffer an educated guess if they are not certain. Doing so will show them that not answering correctly will not result in punitive actions or an otherwise negative impact on their course grade. Rather, your encouragement and support may result in the student developing sufficient trust and comfort to provide an answer, even if it is not correct. Still other students will respond to your questions and do well, suggesting that they had read the assigned materials. If this is the case, give these students a little extra public praise, as doing so will help to reinforce your expectations for readiness for the group as a whole.

Reading checklist

▶ Is the reading material at the right level?

▶ Is it the right length?

▶ Is the material current?

▶ Does it include primary sources?

▶ Is the reading easily accessible?

▶ How well does the reading material lend itself to discussion?

▶ Do the reading assignments conflict with university holidays?

▶ Have you secured the required copyrights?

Recommended readings

It is also advisable during the preparation of your syllabus that you include some recommended readings to supplement the core assigned readings. This will provide your best students with some resources for further investigation and analysis. Further, by providing your students with some contextual notes, as opposed to a list of books or articles, you can whet their appetite even further.

Example

For some additional examples of political realism, see ...

Example

To see how interpretations of the Italian Renaissance have evolved over time, compare reading X with readings Y and Z.

Example

This reading has long been considered the most important text in the field of Developmental Psychology.

Recommended readings can also provide your students a useful starting point for research purposes for longer written assignments. Remember, the list of recommended readings does not need to be voluminous. In fact, an overly-long recommended reading list may actually discourage your students by making them feel overwhelmed, or possibly intimidated. If they are writing a research paper for your class, they may even conclude that it is necessary to pad their own bibliography.

Recommended discussion questions

In preparing your syllabus, you should always include some recommended issues for discussion for each particular class session. These discussion questions will help to 'cue' your students on what is really important for the class, and thereby reinforce the class objectives.

Example

The author lists four reasons why students drop out of education prior to graduation. Can you think of any additional reasons?

Example

What are some of the distinguishing characteristics of adult learners?

Since the questions are designed to facilitate discussion, you should avoid developing any that could be answered with a simple 'yes' or 'no' response. Instead, they should be somewhat open-ended and thought-provoking. You should emphasize to your students that the discussion questions are only a point of departure for the seminar.

Initial check of the seminar room

You should make an initial check of your assigned room at least one month prior to the beginning of the course. This should allow you sufficient time to notify maintenance personnel of major mechanical or structural issues that require fixing, such as leaky roofs or inadequate lighting. This initial inspection will give you some ideas on how to develop your seating plan. Your aim is to create a plan that helps to promote the discussion and collaboration consistent with inquiry-based learning.

The seating arrangements: the mechanics

The seating arrangement should mesh well with the audio-visual arrangements in the room. You do not want your students to have to crane their necks or rearrange their seats in order to see the blackboard.

The physical set-up of the seminar room is the key variable. Unless the chairs and desks are bolted to the floor, you should offer some flexibility by shifting the seating arrangement to best promote your course objective. Thus, it is important to review some basic options insofar as seating geometry is concerned.

Seating geometry: rectangular

If you use the rectangular set-up, then you should position yourself at one of the shorter ends, since this placement provides your students with a natural focal point. Likewise, if you use an oval seating arrangement, you should position yourself at one of the narrow ends for the same reason.

Circular and square arrangements

The circular arrangement denies any explicit hierarchy, since everyone is situated equidistant from the centre. The same holds true for square seating arrangements. Unless your seminar is very small (e.g., say, up to six students), you will want to avoid these arrangements. As the seminar leader, you are not just another student. For this reason, you should position yourself in a way that is consistent with your authority as the seminar leader.

Additional seating considerations

The seating arrangements you definitely want to avoid are those that position students so that they cannot see everyone's face. This is, of course, the standard set-up in most lecture-based courses. This type of set-up actually discourages dialogue among the students, since none of the students are actually facing one another. As you will be facing students and, as seminar leader, are the focal point of the session, the result will be that students will more than likely direct comments to you, even if they are meant for someone else.

You do not want to have any overflow seating positions that are set apart from the other students. This creates a default two-tier (or multi-tier) class system which is undesirable, since the geometry implies that some students are positioned to engage while others are situated merely to observe. You should have a seating arrangement that provides equal access and visibility for all your students.

You should consider giving yourself some extra space by repositioning seats to your immediate left and right a little farther away. This will provide you with some extra table space for course materials you may want to reference during class, and give you some extra room to roam in the event you like to stand up on occasion while teaching your seminar.

Seating assignments

The decision to set assigned seats is a judgement call based on a number of factors. Some professors believe it is best to let the students sit wherever they wish. In some cases, this approach may work, especially if the seminar is limited to just a handful of students. But this approach is risky with larger seminars. For instance, the likelihood of needless distractions increases if friends are allowed to sit next to one another.

If you need to create a seating chart, then create it online since it will be easier for you to modify or update if necessary. You will also need to generate placards for the seating chart, taking care to ensure that the text is large enough to read from any point in the seminar room.

Seating charts will help you learn the names of your students early in the semester and will also provide a valuable reference for visitors. You can also provide the seating chart electronically to guest speakers and lecturers. The seating chart should contain essential information, such as names and nationalities.

The creation of a seating chart involves an element of risk. It is always possible that one (or more) students may feel uncomfortable sitting next to a particular student for whatever reason. If a student makes a complaint along these lines, then you should plan on doing your best to accommodate them, either by counselling the offending party or by simply reassigning seats to solve the problem. This rarely happens but, when it does, you should be prepared to intervene.

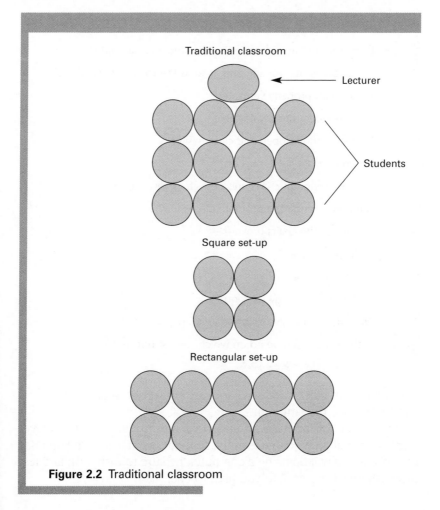

Figure 2.2 Traditional classroom

Final room check

You should make one final check a couple of days before classes begin to ensure everything in the seminar room is in good working order. Walk around the room. Sit down in one of the seats your students will use. Take a deep breath. Swivel. Lean back. Review your checklist one last time.

Yes, checking the room sounds like a mundane, even dreary, chore, and in some ways it is. But this remains an essential preparatory task. There is no faster way to get your course off to a poor start than by being distracted by some problem that could have easily been prevented if you had exercised a little foresight and preparation.

Room checklist:

▶ Is the room clearly identified so the students can find it easily?

▶ Are all the lights working and, if so, is the room sufficiently lit?

▶ Is the room properly ventilated?

▶ Is the temperature comfortable?

▶ Do the windows open and close easily?

▶ Do you need a key for access?

▶ Are there enough chairs and desks for everyone?

▶ Are they arranged to promote discussion?

▶ Are any of the chairs broken?

▶ Is the room clean?

▶ Is there a waste bin?

▶ Is all the technology working?

▶ Does the room have appropriate maps?

▶ Is there a bulletin board on which to post notices?

Is it the type of place conducive to learning? If not, then do what you can to improve the situation.

It is especially important to undertake a thorough test of whatever technology you may wish use in the seminar room before the first day of class. If you will be using a computer, be sure to turn it on and test drive whatever material to you plan to use.

By taking these preparations, you will feel extra confident as your seminar approaches. You can now place your attention where it belongs – on the students!

Reviewing your class roster

You will normally receive a class roster from the registrar's office at least a few days before the seminar begins (if you are lucky, you may receive it even earlier). Most class rosters will contain little more than the most basic information, such as the number of students, their first and last names and year group. From this basic information, you should be able to infer gender and, in most cases, the nationalities of your students.

But even this limited information can help you prepare. You should practice saying the names aloud to become familiar with them. During the initial class session, you should ask the students how they pronounce their names, and if they have any preferred nicknames.

Once you know the number of students, then you can make a final decision as to whether or not to prepare a seating plan. If you begin the course with a seating chart, you may want to give some thought to changing the seating plan part way through the course, or perhaps even doing away with it.

Visualizing success

Psychologists have long recognized the power of imagination when it comes to promoting desired behaviours. Now that you have taken care of all the mechanics of preparing for your seminar, you should spend a few minutes over the course of several days visualizing how you will conduct the seminar. Such mental exercises do not take long and they provide numerous benefits. They can help you imagine both success and failure in the seminar room. By imagining what could go wrong, you can think creatively about how to avoid such problems in the first place. Moreover, by imagining success, the visualization exercises can provide you with an extra dose of confidence as you prepare for your course.

Imagine yourself leading the seminar with poise and confidence. You lead your students in an insightful and creative dialogue, enjoying with them the joy of collaborative, inquiry-based learning. All your students are alert, curious and eager to contribute to the dialogue. Your questions stimulate their thinking and spike their curiosity in ways they never thought possible. They contribute with their own analysis and questions, feeding off your enthusiasm for the subject matter and love of teaching. Before you know it, the seminar is ended. As always with a great seminar, the demand for further discussion far outruns the available supply of time. You and your students depart the seminar room feeling energized and eager to prepare for the next seminar.

This is the type of seminar you want to visualize well before the actual seminar begins. Such mental dress rehearsals will help to prime you for peak performance in the seminar room.

▶ Summary

Proper seminar preparation involves immense effort: there is no doubt about that. It also requires close attention to detail. Does my syllabus have the correct page numbers? Are the hotlinks to the readings all working? Have I ordered enough books for the class? Details left unattended or uncorrected tend to become increasingly irritating and distracting, like a pebble in your shoe.

The pay-off for advanced and detailed preparation is high for educators. As emphasized in this chapter, your confidence level will increase in tandem with your preparation. Preparation is, in fact, the best antidote to nerves. Moreover, with such preparation your seminar is far more likely to get off to a strong start and will be better positioned to make mid-course corrections, if required.

In some sports, it is not uncommon for athletes to remark how much tougher practices are than actual matches. The emphasis on practice is by design, since it increases the chances of a successful season. As seminar leader, you should adopt the same mentality with your preparation: prepare early and often so that you are primed for executing your course as thoroughly and smoothly as possible.

KEY CHAPTER TAKEAWAYS

▶ Test drive everything you will use in the seminar room well in advance. This will build your confidence and reduce the potential for glitches by carefully preparing all aspects of your course.

▶ Review your course materials by imagining that you are looking at them through the eyes of a student.

▶ Ensure that your seminar aligns class lessons, themes and course objectives with the broader aims of the department.

▶ Visualize success and thereby enhance your ability to execute a dynamic and stimulating seminar.

▶ Recall that even the best preparation will not eliminate the potential for mistakes during the execution phase. However, it will reduce the odds of making major and preventable mistakes.

3 Introductions and ground rules

It is often said that first impressions tend to be the most enduring. Arthur Schopenhauer's notion that 'It is only at the first encounter that a face makes its full impression on us' is not without merit.

Of all the seminar sessions you will hold, the first is the most important. This first seminar session will set the overall tone for the course and thus play a decisive role in determining the success or failure of all the sessions to follow.

The participant entering the seminar room for the first time will be struck by several things: the arrangement of the chairs and the table, the size of the room, the lighting and general atmosphere. Is the seminar to be small, intimate with few participants in a comfortable setting, or will it be conducted in a cavernous chamber designed to hold a hundred or more students? How are the chairs arranged? Are they in a circle or in the classic flat or tiered row formation facing the seminar leader? The answers to these questions help set the tone for the first meeting. However, these variables are less important than the first impression that you, as seminar leader, make on your participants.

Whether through word of mouth (where critiques of you, the seminar leader, have been passed down from participant to participant, class to class over the months or years that you have led this and/or other seminars), or through unfounded supposition, participants may already have a strong impression of who you are and the type of seminar leader you will be. Such pre-existing notions, whether fair or not, could certainly influence first impressions.

However, the most important moments that will prove enduring are those when participants first meet you. They will immediately note your demeanour and physical appearance, the timbre of your voice, the 'attitude' you project (e.g., serious, friendly, authoritarian, lackadaisical, or sombre). They will pick up on your mood and a make a snap judgement about whether or not the seminar to come will be something to which you and they can look forward.

The goal, then, at the outset, is to create and maintain a sense that this seminar is to be something quite different … something unique.

You want the participants to realize that the seminar will not permit them to sit quietly and just absorb information, taking notes with the intent of passing examinations while otherwise not caring very much about the discussion at hand. Rather, you want your participants to be pleasantly surprised to meet a seminar leader who is welcoming and personable; someone who really seems genuinely enthusiastic and happy to have the students there as participants.

How to accomplish this? One way, if you have not already met participants prior to the seminar, is to position yourself by the main entrance to the seminar room and greet each of the participants as they enter. Look them in the eye, introduce yourself, ask them for their name and shake their hand, ensuring that, from your attitude and friendly approach, they feel welcome and at home in your seminar.

This small but very critical first step may seem anathema to those who place great emphasis on the senior–subordinate relationship between professor and student, which we refer to as the classroom authority gradient.[1] However, in conducting the seminar, your goal is to stimulate thoughtful and creative discourse between you as the leader and the students as participants, as well as between the participants themselves. You may find that, by employing such initial greetings, you have removed some of the behavioural barriers created by the authority gradient, and fostered discussion from those who may not otherwise have actively participated. Of course, there are those participants who will need time before they are willing to engage in open discussion, but at least some will have garnered a first impression from your welcome that what is to come may prove to be of interest.

You may elect not to meet participants upon their entering the seminar for the first time, and would prefer to enter the seminar room once participants have been seated. If this is the case, then another way to help create a positive initial impression (i.e., the foundation of their mental model of you and the seminar to come) is to ensure that, when you are entering the seminar room for the first time, you do so with a confident stride that conveys a sense of purpose. You may well wish to add an affirmative nod of the head and warm smile for good measure. Too often, one will observe instructors entering the room and approaching their desk or a podium with their shoulders slouched, face serious, giving the impression of a sour disposition at worst or indifference at best. They will address participants in an inexpressive or even authoritarian manner that reinforces the classroom authority gradient. Such approaches to a first meeting could foster an immediate impression in participants that is anything but positive. This may set an unfortunate tone that could colour whatever is to follow.

Again, it is critical here to ensure that, from the very first moment, participants know they are welcome, and that you and they will be engaged in a course of study over the next weeks or months that should prove both engaging and rewarding.

▶ Introductions

Whether at the seminar room entrance or within, the students have already started building their 'mental model'; they have some initial impressions. How, then, should you, as seminar leader, get it all started? There will certainly be some administrative matters to cover with the participants, but it is vital to get to the heart of the seminar right away ... the 'admin' can wait a moment or two. Although you may have already welcomed each student at the seminar room entrance, now is the time to greet everyone as a group, so the participants can get to know one another.

Scan the group of participants, making eye contact with as many as possible. Whatever else may be on your mind at the moment, whether good or not, 'compartmentalize' those items for later reference. Your task for the next hour or so is this seminar ... nothing else should distract you from the participants. You are now on a stage; you are the centre of their attention. Participants will be looking to you to create the scene, direct the play, and lead from the outset.

Your welcome should be heartfelt and cordial – not contrived, or having an air of countless repetition. Greet your participants enthusiastically without becoming too familiar. Your first words will be critical in this regard. Let all participants know that they are welcome. Introduce yourself, describing a bit about your background. You may have this information on a faculty website or in an organizational handbook. You can direct participants to these for further information.

Next, provide participants with a brief overview about the intent of the seminar, the nature and scope of the materials to be covered, and what your goals as seminar leader may be. This will build on whatever they may already know about the seminar. Most critically, it may help undo whatever inaccurate information or false impressions they may have garnered from other students.

After introducing yourself and the seminar, it is time to turn to the participants. It is time to personalize the seminar further by having participants introduce themselves, provided the size of the class is limited to a maximum of no more than 25–30 students. This is not only informative, but also plays the critical role of having participants address you, the seminar leader, as well as the others in the group – something to which some participants may not be accustomed, or be comfortable doing.

As seminar leader, you can dictate the type of information that each participant should provide. Such information may include the following:

- Name
- Home of residence (if an international participant, then country)
- If employed, profession and current job type
- What he or she hopes to gain by attending the seminar
- Outside interests and hobbies
- Anything else he or she would like to share.

It is also helpful (and sometimes revealing) to ask at least one or two follow-up questions of each participant. They can be based on any of the information already provided, or can explore a tangent in which you believe the rest of the participants may have an interest. Doing so demonstrates your personal interest in each of the participants, and provides an effective bridge to open direct conversation between you and each individual. Without using this type of personal interaction, one runs the risk of these first moments in your seminar becoming a sterile, check-the-box affair. Introductions conducted in this manner will help put your participants more at ease – and you may learn some more interesting things about your participants.

There are variations on this theme that you may wish to use. For example, rather than asking students to make their introductions themselves, you may wish to have them introduce themselves to another student, who will, in turn, introduce that individual to the class. Such an approach can make it easier for students to get to know one other in a more direct yet informal manner. It can also reduce the possibility that some students may talk too much or too little about themselves.

Whatever your approach, it is critical that you pay close attention to these introductions. Take brief notes so that you will remember key points that may be useful to recall in subsequent discussions.

▶ Personalize the seminar: name tags and tents

The seminar leader and participants should learn each other's names fairly early during the seminar process, as they will be addressing one another frequently. One way to facilitate this process would be by providing name tags and/or name tents. Name tags should be worn for at least the first few meetings. If participants are seated at desks or tables, their name tent is placed before them in such a manner so that other participants are able to read their names easily.

The first day is the best time for the seminar participants to double-check their name tags and name tents for any inadvertent mistakes so that corrected replacements can be provided as soon as practicable.

In addition to identifying the participants, the name tents tradition-ally serve to indicate the participants' desire to speak when placed in a vertical position. This time-tested technique allows the seminar leader to direct conversational traffic more easily and saves your participants the trouble of holding their arms aloft while waiting for a chance to speak. You may elect to permit free discourse without requiring partic-ipants to signal in some way that they wish to speak. However, without using such 'signals', you may find that participants interrupt or 'step on' the narratives of others. The use of name tents as signals indicat-ing the desire to speak thus provides a non-intrusive means of ensur-ing that all contributing participants are recognized and called on.

In this regard, the exercise of respect during the conduct of the seminar should begin with how one should address participants. In some environments where seminar discourse is maintained at an informal level, it may be considered acceptable for the seminar leader to address participants by their first name. Despite permitting this level of informality, proper decorum and respect should be main-tained between participants and the seminar leader. As such (unless otherwise expressly instructed by the leader), participants should address seminar leaders not as peers but by their family name.

In other environments, addressing students by their first names only would be considered most inappropriate. It is up to you, the seminar leader, to decide how participants and you are to be addressed. One helpful general rule of thumb in this regard is that, in seminars where participants represent different age groups and cultures, it is recommended that they be addressed in a more formal manner; that is, by family name.

▶ Basic ground rules

There may be many participants who have not attended a seminar before. It would therefore be helpful to take some minutes during your first meeting to explain to your participants how exactly this particular forum differs from other modes of instruction; specifically, the types of formal lectures to which most seminar participants are accustomed.

For the majority of participants, formal lectures are inherently passive learning experiences. The expectations are clear: the lecturer provides information and the participant receives it. While an interactive environment, many formal lectures (especially those that are popular or required) are attended by large numbers of students and are held in large classrooms or auditorium-like facilities. Time constraints and the numbers of attendees mean that only a small percentage of participants will be able to take advantage of the opportunity for questions and answers during the course of, or after the completion of, the lecture.

While they lack the formality of a lecture, seminar discussions are inherently active forums that, while encouraging open, ongoing interactions between participants and seminar leader as well with each other, should nonetheless focus on specific learning objectives. This is facilitated through the restriction or limiting of the number of participants permitted to attend a given seminar. As a function of their small size and free-exchange of ideas, seminars can and should be lively at times. However, by virtue of their structure and goal-directed approaches, seminars must never be confused with even less-formal group discussions that often take place outside the classroom and in online chat rooms.

Punctuality

Punctuality, both on the part of the seminar leader as well as the participants, is a professional norm that needs to be emphasized strongly and enforced from the first day of the seminar; doing so helps set the tone for serious discussions to follow.

As seminar leader, it is strongly recommended that you be present at the seminar venue prior to the start of the meeting, both to greet participants and to prepare your seminar presentation materials. Doing so not only reminds participants of the critical nature of time in seminar scheduling, but also provides them with the possibility of chatting with you informally prior to the start of the seminar. This type of interaction (along with office hours and after-hours social events, if appropriate) can give both you and participants the opportunity to interact beyond the limited block of time allotted to the seminar itself.

Make your intent as to punctuality clear to participants attending this first meeting of the seminar. Stress the notions that tardiness not only disrupts the flow of the seminar, but also that such behaviour deprives the rest of the participants with what could prove to be informative contributions by those committing such misdemeanours.

One very effective technique to help promote punctuality is simply to begin speaking at the designated start time regardless of whether or not the room is quiet, or even if all the seminar participants have not yet arrived. There is no need to shout, though raising your voice a notch may help. Most participants will see that you are ready to begin; often a couple of participants will assume the role of enforcers on your behalf, asking those still talking to be quiet.

Starting on time provides a powerful incentive for seminar participants to arrive at the seminar a few minutes early; failing to do so could (and usually does) result in some embarrassment, as other participants will make note of the late arrivals … a practice made even more effective if you pause in your narrative until the tardy arrival has taken his or her seat. Depending on the circumstances and the nature of seminar participants, repeat offenders can be taken aside in private and be reminded as to the importance of punctuality.

Bringing the seminar session to a punctual close also requires a sense of tact and diplomacy. As seminar leader, you would never wish to cut off a participant in mid-sentence during the seminar period, notwithstanding the importance of ending on time. The way to avoid this outcome is to close the discussion a few minutes early and leave time to provide seminar participants with guidance on future assignments, make administrative announcements, or provide some preliminary remarks about the next seminar.

It is imperative that you keep close track of the time in order to manage the seminar discussion. The seminar room must have a timepiece mounted on a wall, a podium or other location, easily visible to both you and participants. You should include this requirement as part of your preparations prior to the start of the first meeting. If your seminar venue lacks a clock, be certain to see to it that one is provided. In this regard, if it is at all possible, try to avoid repeatedly looking at your wristwatch. Some seminar participants may interpret this gesture as boredom, nervousness, or possible disinterest on your part, regardless of your intent. As a seminar leader observing this behaviour from participants, you would probably come to the same – perhaps erroneous, yet nevertheless disconcerting – conclusions.

No use of electronics for personal reasons

In the modern learning environment, one notes the plethora of electronic equipment being employed by students and participants. Some use it to facilitate learning (such as the taking of notes), while others use it for purposes other than those associated with the seminar. It is imperative that there be no distractions during the seminar; nothing to draw the attention of participants (and seminar leaders) away from the discourse at hand. Ringing and buzzing cell phones, laptop computers with access to the internet, devices that provide the ability to email and/or otherwise send texts to others are all sources of distraction that, if permitted during the seminar, can severely disrupt ongoing discourse.

It is therefore imperative that, during the opening moments of your first seminar meeting, you explain why the use of personal electronic devices (cell phones, pagers, and so on) is not permitted in the seminar room at any time. All such devices should be turned off, or placed in standby mode prior to the start of the seminar.

Instructors should use their discretion in deciding whether or not the use of personal computing devices with access to the internet should be permitted during the seminar period. For students, such devices can be very helpful for note-taking. Further, an instructor may wish that students access the internet in order to reference information sources appropriate to the discussion at hand. However, students should be informed that access to computer-based activities other than those associated with the seminar is not permitted while the seminar is in progress.

Most participants will not openly object to this policy; those that do should be reminded about the necessity for undivided attention during the seminar.

Non-attribution policy

Interestingly, one of the reasons that a participant may not wish to voice their thoughts or opinions actively during the course of a discussion is due to the fear or concern that what they state may be in some way held against them; that they (or those with whom they are associated professionally or personally) could be personally accountable for a belief, opinion, or action that may be considered controversial to some and unacceptable to others. The result may be that these participants may elect to not interact with others during the discussion at hand; sitting quietly and unproductively while others carry on.

One way to counter this problem is through the implementation of what is termed a 'non-attribution policy'. A non-attribution policy provides both faculty and participants with the freedom to voice their opinions without fear of repercussion or attribution. It is a binding covenant with the participants that all discussions will be treated as privileged information. In practical terms, 'non-attribution' means it is permissible for seminar participants to tell other participants in the course (or anyone outside the course, for that matter) that they discussed topics A, B and C in seminar, but not attribute any of the discussed ideas or positions to a particular participant. All participants should be made aware of this policy during the first meeting. Further, all visitors and guest speakers whom you may invite to attend your seminar should be reminded of this non-attribution policy. This will encourage them to be as a candid as possible when they engage your seminar participants.

Visitors

It is critical to exercise caution with regard to inviting visitors or observers to attend your seminar. In some cases, they may be special guests whom you have invited to participate in discussions of particular topics. In other cases, they may be colleagues or other members of your institution/organization, or even from outside your organization who have requested permission to sit in on, but not actively participate in, one or more of your seminars. Be aware that their presence may or may not impact the tone and content of the discussions at hand. Participants will be aware of their presence and may even feel intimidated to the point that they refrain from voicing their opinions.

Further, if topics are sensitive, such visitors may not feel compelled to adhere to your stated non-attribution policy, the results of which could yield unexpected and possibly unwelcome outcomes for you and/or the participants. As seminar leader, you should take these notions into serious consideration prior to granting approval for seminar attendance by non-participants.

Seminar bonding

Your efforts to set the proper tone for the seminar can contribute to what is known as seminar 'bonding'; that is, your close interaction with participants both during and outside the allotted block of seminar time. To the extent that your seminar permits, and as appropriate, you should make every effort to promote and participate in seminar-related activities outside the seminar room. Such activities or events may include field trips and outings, visits to meet individuals or groups at other facilities, attendance at lectures or other seminars that are in some way related to your own seminar topic(s) or theme(s), cultural pursuits and even sporting events. These activities are not only enjoyable for their own sake, but they can also help to promote the creation of a distinct seminar team identity. This cohesiveness, in turn, can foster positive seminar interaction and enhanced learning opportunities upon return to the academic setting.

The programming of such additional events should be outlined during the first meeting. Participants should be strongly encouraged to attend these activities. However, they should not be subject to penalties if there are factors that, on occasion, preclude their being able to do so.

Civility in the seminar room

One of the seminar ground rules must therefore be that all discussions are to take place in an atmosphere of mutual respect and civility. As noted earlier, there may be times during the course of the seminar that discussions associated with strongly-held personal attitudes, opinions and beliefs may become quite impassioned. During such times, some of your participants may become so disengaged from acceptable civil discourse that their interaction with others may potentially devolve to a point that it could become disruptive. The defence of strongly-held beliefs is to be encouraged, but participants must remember that all discourse must be couched in the tenets of the seminar: that is, thoughtful and constructive with respect to other participants.

The seminar leader should emphasize this imperative during the initial seminar and remind all participants of this requirement as often as necessary during meetings thereafter. In this regard, the seminar leader could inform participants of this ground rule in the following manner: 'Let's keep our seminar discussions at a high level. We will and should have vigorous, even spirited, discussions. But personal attacks will not be allowed.'

If a seminar participant crosses the line and makes an inappropriate comment, you should first give the participant the opportunity to clarify or retract the remarks by saying something like, 'John, perhaps I misunderstood what you were trying to say. Did you really mean to say that (insert narrative in question here)? Please clarify for us.'

It is important here to note that the consequences of a seminar leader breaking a ground rule are severe and far-reaching. The leader must be the guide, the authority who lives by the ground rules that he or she implements and enforces. It takes only one breach of this tenet to destroy the credibility of a seminar leader, who must remain accountable for his or her responsibilities at all times. This does not imply that seminar leaders cannot express opinions that they may embrace. However, such opinions openly expressed by the seminar leader have the potential, even inadvertently, to add a level of bias to all future sessions. Participants may either be reluctant, or refuse, to discuss issues frankly and in a manner that they (mistakenly) believe may result in some sort of punitive action being taken by the seminar leader (i.e., lowering of a course grade).

It is therefore imperative that seminar leaders monitor and temper their own discussion content so as to ensure that their words do not produce even the perception of bias, especially with respect to sensitive and controversial topics. They should guide the discussion towards a particular goal and at a high level of intellectual discourse. Also, seminar leaders must always remember that, despite the non-attribution ground rule being in place, ultimately they are the authority and their words will, rightly or wrongly, have great influence on the participants, for which the leaders can be held accountable.

▶ After the first meeting

You have held your first seminar session … a big hurdle, especially if this was your first time leading a seminar. The students are gone; the seminar room is empty; now it would be prudent to spend some time thinking about how you believe it all went.[2]

You may have a multitude of questions running through your mind at this point, some constructive and some, perhaps, even destructive. Constructively, you may be asking yourself:

* *Did I accomplish all that I wanted to do?*

The syllabus provides an overview of those topics to be covered during the course of the seminar. The amount of time you have during each seminar period is limited and should be strictly enforced. You should therefore time yourself, pacing your discussion and that of your students such that you are able to meet the goal(s) of the seminar meeting. This approach should be taken during all seminar meetings, the tone of which can be set at this first encounter with your students. If, at the end of the meeting, you find that you were unable to cover all that you had hoped, you should ask yourself why. Were discussions lengthy, irrelevant and poorly directed? Were there distractions that pulled you and the students away from the topics at hand? It is critical to find that delicate balance between allowing ongoing discourse and providing time-paced direction to the flow of such discourse, ensuring that the topics of the day are covered, but allowing for some flexibility in your scheduling.

* *Did the students seem interested in what was being discussed?*

How could you tell? There are several ways to know if your students were attuned to the discussions at hand. Some are obvious: Did they answer your questions? Did they engage in discussion with each other as well as with you, the seminar leader? Were the students attentive, or did one or more seem distracted, uninterested?

Usually, most students will be assessing the instructor during this first meeting. They will be making some decisions about you and the topics at hand that they will carry throughout the remainder of the seminar (see discussion on first impressions on pp. 32–4). As a result, students will attend to what you have to say. They will be interested in more than hearing about course content; they will also be watching you for your style, body language, your approach to teaching and general appeal. As a result, they may be attending to you during the course of this first meeting.

* *Do you think the students are looking forward to the seminar meetings to follow?*

You will be watching the students as they leave the seminar room, listening to their informal banter with one another, trying to find some clue as to their thoughts about the first meeting and what is to come. These may be moments not very well spent, however. For, unless you provide a written critique to be filled out anonymously, it will not be an easy task to gauge student attitudes after this first meeting.

Remember, that the primary intent of the first session is to introduce yourself and to let the students do the same, and to describe the nature and scope of the seminar in such a way as to stimulate the interest in your students for what is to come. In this regard, you may even have left the topic 'hanging' somewhat at the close of the first session, promising to address certain themes or answering 'hot issue' questions at the second meeting – essentially, making them wish to return to the seminar room to see what is to happen next. This strategy has long been successfully employed by most successful authors of thriller novels.

- *What are my own first impressions about the students?*

Not only might you be wondering what your students think about you, you will also have some first impressions about the students, both individually and as a group. Certain students will clearly show an interest in the seminar; especially, those sitting in seats closest to the front, and responding eagerly and frequently, might elicit a positive first impression. You might have the impression that some seem less than attentive to the proceedings and, as such, might elicit a negative first impression. Others may seem attentive but appear loath to take an active role in the discussions. You might hold your impressions somewhat in abeyance, waiting to assess their performance during subsequent meetings. What one must avoid here is allowing first impressions to carry over to your interactions with students during the sessions that follow. Student attitude and performance are dynamic and can change over the course of the seminar due to a plethora of personal variables. It is thus a best practice to set aside your own first impressions about individual students as quickly as possible.

- *Are there ways that I can improve this session the next time the seminar is being held?*

This is probably the most important of all the constructive questions you could ask yourself after the first session. If you believe that there are certain aspects of the first session that can be improved, then note them for future reference. Their application, along with critiques offered by students, could prove invaluable to you in the conduct not only of the first meeting, but also of all meetings during current and future seminars.

It is unfortunately part of our nature that we may also dwell on questions that may prove less than constructive – perhaps, even destructive. They generally centre on one's need for affirmation and may include questions such as: What do the students think of me? Do the students like me? Did I verbally stumble or make any errors? Was I boring? As one is not able to ask such questions of the students themselves, these types of self-assessing queries may not be based on accurate perspectives but, rather, on variables associated with a seminar leader's own personality – the discussion of which is beyond the scope of this narrative. In general, such psychodynamic-based inquiry should be avoided if possible, for it may not accurately reflect the state of the seminar leader–student relationship and, as such, can negatively impact one's subsequent interactions with seminar participants.

The key here is to be a constructive seminar leader; one who, by understanding the dynamics of student–seminar leader expectations and by employing various techniques to build and maintain ongoing open discourse, can effectively guide the course of this, the first, and all subsequent seminar meetings. We will discuss these expectations and some of these techniques in Chapter 4.

▶ Summary

First impressions tend to be the most lasting, and this notion holds true when leading a seminar. In this chapter, we have seen that how you start the seminar at that first meeting has the potential to have great influence on subsequent student participation. Taking time during the first meeting to introduce yourself to students and to get to know who they are is one very important way to facilitate the creation and maintenance of 'seminar bonding' – the creative and free exchange of information between yourself and your seminar students.

It is critical from the outset to set the tone of the seminar; to provide students with an idea of the form and style that the seminar is to take. As such, students must be made aware of your desire to have a constructive exchange of ideas unhampered by bias and without fear of attribution. The first meeting should therefore concentrate on setting forth ground rules associated with the conduct of the seminar, especially with regard to the nature of civil discourse. As this chapter has made clear, your goal during this first meeting is to not only create a positive mindset in your students about the seminar itself, but also to also stimulate their interest in what is to come.

KEY CHAPTER TAKEAWAYS

► A strong start to the seminar will create positive momentum for the rest of the semester (term); a weak start can be overcome, but at a high cost of time and effort.

► It is essential that all your students understand the seminar ground rules for discussion.

► The power of example is vital for setting standards and norms in the seminar room. Display the behaviour you expect from your students.

► It is important to convey administrative information to your students during the first couple of class sessions. However, it is far more important to set the tone in terms of your expectations for civil discourse.

► Make your students feel at home in the seminar. If they are not comfortable with you or their classmates, it is unlikely that they will contribute to the ensuing discussions.

4 Create a positive learning cycle

Imagine that you have completed the first meeting of your seminar. All seems to have gone well. You said all you had to say, covering the topics outlined in the syllabus for that day. The students were not very responsive, nor were there very many questions asked, but you reassure yourself that that's all right; this was just the first day of the seminar and most were probably somewhat uncomfortable or unsure of the situation. Seeking to reassure yourself that they will certainly relax and become more engaged as the seminar continues, you begin preparing for the next seminar session.

You may be right in your optimistic projection – sometimes it does take students a while to loosen up and contribute to seminar discussion. But the more likely trajectory here is potentially quite negative, since you have minimized the importance of the first session and its less than satisfactory outcomes.

You are well aware that a negative environment combined with poor teaching techniques can prove disastrous in the lecture hall. So it is with seminars as well, where ineffective or inadequate seminar leadership can (and will) dissuade participation, and undermine the learning benefits normally associated with inquiry-based learning and Socratic discourse. If this negative dynamic is left unchecked, the seminar participation will steadily diminish and the seminar will degenerate into an exercise in wasted time. When interaction diminishes, the leader assumes the role of lecturer and communication becomes progressively more one-sided.

A vicious cycle is now in full swing; the instructor solicits responses and there are few or none. With each attempt to do so, the one-way relationship solidifies into a wall between you and your students that is very difficult to breach. In such a state, it is far more difficult to know if anything has been learned at all in the seminar room.

Your goal then, as a seminar leader, is to create a positive learning cycle, whereby learning is both collaborative and enjoyable. In this regard, it is difficult to overstate the importance of the first couple of seminars in your course. Positive facilitation skills in these early sessions will set the momentum and tone for the entire course. In this regard, they may also preempt many possibly insurmountable problems that could otherwise occur later in the course.

How, then, does one create and maintain this positive learning cycle anew? Let's start by examining the many responsibilities you have as a seminar leader and the expectations that both you and your students have of each other and the seminar.

It is critical at this juncture to remember that you are both the seminar leader and facilitator. In your leadership role, you will direct the course of the seminar from beginning to end. You will provide the topical foundation on which the discussions will be built. You will also probably be preparing, administering and assessing various means to assess student performance that (more often than not) in the end translate into a course grade. Students will more than likely look to you for guidance regarding seminar topics, grades or other concerns.

Recall from Chapter 1, however, that, by design, the seminar is to be a highly interactive environment wherein students will be encouraged to play active roles in the discussions and (as appropriate) debates. This will be your task as a seminar facilitator; the active promotion of open, frank discussion and the guidance of it in such a manner that it contributes to the topic(s) at hand. It is therefore critical that you, as the seminar leader, also possess the acumen to facilitate such discourse. Doing so may not prove as simple or easy as you may expect, however; to do so effectively requires a fine blend of patience, tact, diplomacy and resolve – the latter to ensure that the discussion remains relevant and even-handed. With this in mind, it is important to reflect on whether or not you believe you are, or can be, a good seminar facilitator.

A good way to begin this self-assessment is to start with a review of the nature of facilitation in general and how it can be both positive (constructive) as well as negative (destructive).

▶ The nature of facilitation

There are three principle variables that have been commonly applied to the hiring practices and that can be herein associated with seminar leadership competency: knowledge, skills and abilities.[1] For reasons that will soon become apparent, all three are necessary for effective seminar facilitation. Let us address each of these in turn.

Knowledge

This first variable defines whether or not the seminar leader possesses a firm academic (theoretical and/or applied) background associated with the topic(s) being discussed. Keeping in mind that one of the leader's roles in a seminar is to be a subject matter expert, students will give little credence to seminar leaders with little foundation in the discipline in which they are presumed to be an expert.

That said, the expectation of subject matter expertise does not imply that the seminar leader can, and will be able to, answer all questions and concerns that could arise during the course of discussion. However, a knowledgeable seminar leader will likely know how best to access resources designed to address these unanswered questions. Depending on the complexity and difficulty of the question, the seminar leader may want to research the answer directly; in which case, this is best done at the start of the next seminar session, prior to addressing issues already scheduled for that particular day. Alternatively, the seminar leader could perhaps point the student towards resources that will answer the question.

Skills

Facilitation skills can be thought of as those seminar participant-directed rules, strategies and actions a seminar leader uses to foster open, ongoing intellectual discourse between the participants themselves and with the leader. These strategies and actions guide the path of the seminar such that all participants have opportunities to play active roles in the discourse at hand. Such skills are usually developed over time and with experience.

The notion that anyone is able to stand in front of a group of individuals and easily conduct a seminar, promoting discussions, providing information in a stimulating and erudite manner, is clearly misplaced. While some seminar leaders appear to be at ease in front of groups with a 'stage presence' that enables them to easily relate with their 'audience', there are others who are clearly ill at ease when addressing such groups. Their speech is not always clear, they appear nervous as they fidget, not quite knowing what to do with their hands. Their tone and timbre of speech are stilted, curt and monotonous. They tend to shield themselves behind podiums, continuously consulting a wall clock or their wristwatch, appearing to read from their notes rather than engaging students directly. Others may show a reluctance or inability to field questions from students; either they hesitate to answer, or provide answers that are inadequate.

All of this sounds pretty awful, but most of us have at some time encountered such seminar leaders or instructors during the course of our education. What is critical here is that these characteristics are not to be misconstrued as inherent faults; rather, they are indicators that an instructor may not have developed or employed the skills associated with successful seminar leadership. More on this in a moment.

Abilities

This variable concerns whether or not an individual possesses the physical and emotional bearing to lead a seminar. The physical dimension is the less important of the two, as physical capabilities do not necessarily correlate with one's ability to carry out the responsibilities of seminar leader. Those individuals with the knowledge and skills required for carrying out a seminar will find that most physical limitations will in no way impair their ability to do so.

The emotional component is far more important, since it shapes and influences behaviour in determining whether an individual tends to be intolerant, unforgiving, arrogant, narcissistic, extremely argumentative, unable to delegate responsibility to others: such an individual may not be best able to lead a group of students in open discussion or debate. Similarly, individuals who are hesitant in their effective direction (management) of a group, who may feel threatened by debate, or who may lack the stamina or willpower to directly engage with their students may also not be able to carry out the responsibilities of a seminar leader.

One may possess both the knowledge and skills to do so, but still lack the ability, while one may have the ability and knowledge but not the skills. Thus, it is important that all three variables together should be borne in mind when considering the areas requiring improvement in order for an individual to be a successful seminar leader.

► Positive facilitation

Let us assume that an individual preparing to become a seminar leader will have the requisite knowledge and abilities to do so. However, this handbook is based on the notion that not everyone may have the skills, or that, even if they do, they may not know how to put them to effective use in seminar leadership. It is therefore best at this point to describe some of these 'positive' facilitation skills; those that would, when employed, create an effective, positive seminar environment for both students and seminar leaders.

Create and adhere to a faculty–participant covenant

An unwritten contract governs faculty–participant discourse in the seminar room. As in every academic situation, all members of the faculty, whether leading or assisting with the seminar, will at all times adhere to ethical guidelines and strictures. As such, you must ensure that, during the course of study, discussions and debate, all participants will be treated fairly and with respect.

It is possible that, in discussions regarding very sensitive topics, verbal exchange can become intense and somewhat emotionally charged. As seminar leader, it will therefore also be your responsibility to guide the discussion in such a manner so as to ensure that all participants exercise appropriate emotional restraint while, at the same time, challenging them intellectually within this basic framework.

For their part, participants must pledge to take the work seriously, and to prepare for and actively participate in the seminar discussions. They also must commit to respect one another's opinions, however different they may be from their own. As noted above, this can be a daunting task, especially when the focus of the discussion is on a topic of great political or moral import to the participant. As seminar leader, you must convey to the participants that either retaining or changing their views should not be seen as a sign of intellectual or moral weakness; rather, defending ones views in a cogent logical manner is a sign of intellectual maturity, as is altering one's views after some discernment. Participants must also know from the start that although their initial worldview on entering the seminar may or may not change by the end of the course of discussion, these views, as well as the assumptions that underlie them, should and will be challenged and tested.

While this faculty–participant covenant is normally unwritten, this does not mean it should be left unsaid. Your syllabus and introductory remarks should outline to the students what this covenant actually means in practice.

▶ Set realistic expectations for both yourself and your students

The role of expectations and the leadership dynamics associated with them can greatly influence the success of your seminar. Expectations can be considered as *a priori* set levels of achievement or goals that (depending on whether or not they are met) may support and/or reinforce one's mental model. If one expects that a vanilla ice cream will look and taste like vanilla, and it does, then the expectation is affirmed and the mental model reinforced. However, if one is given a vanilla ice cream and it looks and tastes like chocolate, then the expectation is not met and the mental model is altered or collapses; the result of which can be confusion, disillusionment and negative behaviour.

It may be that, in the course of designing your seminar, you made assumptions about your students (their capabilities, limitations, interests in the seminar, level of active participation, and so on) that, even after conducting the first seminar session, are at odds with what has actually transpired. That is, these assumptions lead to the creation of expectations and a mental model of how the first session (as well as the remainder of the seminar) would be. If, however, you were not able to cover all that you had wished, or if only a few (if any) participants engaged in discussion, or if it appeared that students were not understanding what you were saying, then these expectations would be violated, possibly resulting in the development of less-than-accurate mental models regarding yourself, your students and/or the seminar in general. Should the impacts of this result be enduring, they may even manifest themselves in subsequent seminar sessions.

It is therefore critical that you, as the seminar leader, create realistic goals for yourself and your students. If these goals cannot be met, then it will be necessary realign these expectations to the dynamics of the seminar; that is, to meet your responsibilities as leader, as well as the needs of your participants. This may require you to remain flexible and adaptable, ensuring that your mental model of the seminar remains dynamic and always employing a constructive approach.

If you see that you are unable to meet some of the expectations for a given seminar period, then adjust them in a manner that is both creative and instructive. This does not necessitate that you decrease the level of quality or scope of information discussed; rather, it may require you to tailor the discussion so as to better fit the time allotted. In doing so, you may be even raising the bar a little, allowing students to attain a higher or more in-depth level of understanding than had originally been expected. In such a case, the mental model is not only reinforced, but also even enhanced through this constructive approach to facilitation.

If you find that the amount or depth of discourse by participants is not meeting your expectations, then despairing at what you may perceive to be your students' failings will only deepen the chasm created by your unfulfilled expectations. The reality could be that you, for any number of reasons, are not affirming the expectations that your students may have had regarding you and/or the seminar. This collision of mental models can only prove destructive.

Clearly, then, it is necessary to ensure that the expectations that you and your students have be as aligned as possible. One way to accomplish this is to ask your students to provide you with a few sentences about what expectations they may have of the seminar. They can do this as part of the biographical narrative that they provide either prior to or during the first seminar period. It would also be helpful to you if, during a meeting at the mid-point in the course of the seminar, they once again provide you with a response to the same question. Still another approach to gathering this information would be to provide your seminar students with the opportunity to give a brief critique of each seminar meeting, noting what they believed to be positive and negative aspects of the meeting, and providing comments to help improve the seminar. You may wish to include a question about expectations as part of this critique. Such critiques should be provided anonymously either via standardized template forms in hard copy, or as part of your seminar online website (Chapter 10 will cover assessments in greater detail).

With this updated information, you can quickly identify whether or not student expectations (and resulting mental models) may have changed over time and, if so, whether in a positive or negative direction. If negative, this information would alert you to the need to address these issues in a quick and effective manner, so as to best facilitate improvement of subsequent seminar meetings.

▶ Assess and, if necessary, refine your presentation skills

How well do you make presentations? Are you happy with your current presentation style? How do you come across to your students? Are you comfortable speaking to and leading groups? Are you able to guide conversation in such a manner as to address specific goals that you have set? Are you amenable to heated discourse on topics that could prove sensitive and emotional, as well as thought-provoking? Are you willing to tailor your approach to presenting information to best meet the needs of your students? These are but some of the questions you should be asking yourself for, as a seminar leader, you will be encountering these as well as a host of other issues defining the roles and relationships between you and your students.

Returning to our opening scenario, recall that you had few real expectations for your first meeting; you really wanted to introduce yourself and let your students do so as well. You also wanted to outline the script (syllabus) that the seminar would be following, including what would be required of participants. You may also have expected (hoped) that some of your students would immediately become active and engaged in discussion. You may even have asked for any questions and, receiving none, you inferred that all had gone fairly well for this first meeting. You expected to present the syllabus for the first meeting within the time allotted and, having done so, you were glad to have met that expectation. You are not certain what expectations your students had for this meeting but, as they seemed alert and attentive, you assumed that whatever they may have been, those expectations had been met.

You may also believe that the manner and style with which you made presentations went well; that you imparted what needed to be known and it was then up to those listening to you to comprehend and respond if necessary. You do not believe that you may not have been understood by some of your students; if that were the case, they would have asked you questions; however, as they did not do so, all must be well. You are therefore quite happy with the way you present yourself and your information. If problems exist, the fault must lie with the students.

If you believe all of this to be so, then you may be making massive – and, potentially, tragically inaccurate – assumptions. You are couching your approach to providing instruction and leadership from an inward-looking perspective, possibly addressing your own needs and expectations at the cost of those of your students. For instance, as none of the seminar participants are requesting clarity, then you assume that you are necessarily being understood. However, there are many reasons that students may not be coming to you for clarity

– anything from complacency, to feeling it inappropriate to admit to not understanding what you have said, to fear of being thought of as inadequate. It may also be the case that students are reluctant to question you as an authority, even after you have assured them that it is, at times, appropriate and necessary to do so.

It is best, then, to ensure that you follow some basic guidelines in conducting your seminar in this first and all subsequent meetings so that the students are comfortable asking you for clarification when needed. Here, then, are some tips that you may find useful to put into practice from the very beginning.

- *It is important that you address your seminar participants in a manner so as not to appear threatening or arrogant.*

Remember, you are not there to lecture. As such, you seek to facilitate and guide, not stifle, discourse. Your demeanour must therefore be welcoming and open. This means you should seek to engage your students on the level of participant-to-participant; it is critical that your role as leader be recognized. But, if the manner and style with which you present information is somewhat relaxed, then it will be easier for you engage your students in collaborative learning.

- *You should show an unswerving interest in what your students have to say, regardless of whether or not you agree with them.*

Taking this one step further, you should be tactful in how you guide them should they become mired in an irrelevant or unanswerable point. Should they pursue a line that is inappropriate to a discussion, you should redirect the discourse, but do so in a way that does not seem patronizing or otherwise demeaning.

Example

Negative (destructive) facilitation:

Jim, your line of thought is confusing and really irrelevant to the topic.

Positive (constructive) facilitation:

Jim, that's an interesting line of thought. Please share with us how you came to your conclusions.

You can see that the destructive approach could cause Jim to be embarrassed or angry, and could lead to his not contributing further to the discussion. Conversely, the constructive tack recognizes what he has said, yet guides him back to the topic at hand in a manner that further encourages Jim's participation.

• *Your information should be presented clearly and concisely, eschewing jargon, undefined acronyms and any other source of possible ambiguity.*

This point is especially critical when having students in your seminar whose first language may not be English. This is a common problem where seminar leaders assume that all participants understand all forms of English, spoken in any type of dialect and at any speed.

This author (Andrew Bellenkes) can recall moving from the northeastern United States down to the Florida panhandle region, not far from Mississippi, Louisiana and Alabama. The various southern dialects and vocal nuances made my understanding of many conversations with those native to these southern states somewhat challenging at first. One can only imagine the challenge this could offer to those seminar participants from non-English speaking countries. The seminar leader should actively concentrate on his or her manner of speaking, ensuring that all words are clearly pronounced and spoken at a speed designed for those who may have some difficulty understanding what you are saying. This does not mean speaking louder or comically slow; it just means being aware of how clear and quickly you are addressing seminar participants. Your students will immediately pick up on the fact that you are willing to adjust your diction for their benefit, and this will help set a positive tone.

In this regard, it is also recommended that you insert a break in your thoughts every so often and ask the participants whether they have understood what you have imparted and whether there are any questions. Such a tactic not only provides for the 'chunking' (rather than continuous flow) of information (which could help learning and retention), but also affords students the opportunity to ask questions or offer feedback that you could, in turn, use to guide the rest of your presentation.

• *Avoid using a podium or lectern as a shield or barrier between you and the seminar participants.*

If the seminar room is limited in size and you only have a very small number of students, then it may be best to situate yourself and your students in a circle. This arrangement will help you stimulate discussion and facilitate participation.

Even with larger groups you should avoid hiding behind a podium or lectern at all costs. This will reduce the temptation to lecture. Rather than remaining in one place when addressing larger seminars, it is recommended that you move about, walking among the students if the seating and seminar room layout permit, continuing to speak while mobile. If a student has a question, or if you wish to address a particular student, it is helpful to walk up to them, not so close as to appear uncomfortably challenging, but sufficiently close to indicate to that student that it is he or she in particular with whom you wish to have a discussion. This tactic is especially useful when engaging students who tend to be passive and unresponsive to questions addressed to the entire group. Walking up to and addressing them in a non-confrontational manner will probably make such students feel comfortable enough to respond.

- *Know your students' backgrounds sufficiently well to draw out their experiences.*

Prior to the first meeting, you may receive contact information for students who will be attending your seminar. Once you have this in hand, it is strongly recommended that, prior to or during the first meeting, you ask all participants to provide you with a paragraph describing themselves in brief, including a sentence or two listing what they seek to get out of the course. With this approach, you will probably find out some useful information about their backgrounds that can then be used to encourage students to comment on a particular topic.

You could say something like, 'Sarah, I believe that you have already had some experience with this particular issue. Have you any thoughts or opinions about this?', or something to that effect. Such a query signals to all of the participants that you have taken the time to learn something about them. Moreover, it also underscores your belief that their expertise or experiences will greatly benefit the discussion – an excellent example of constructive facilitation.

- *Do not read your seminar notes.*

There is nothing worse for those participating in a seminar than to listen to a leader reading from notes. This is the antithesis of inquiry-based learning. The result not only can prove boring, but the reading of notes also precludes the ability of a leader to address participants directly. The leader is concentrating on the notes rather than the students and is thus missing all of the facial expressions and body language critical to the leader knowing whether or not the students are interested in what is being imparted. As mentioned earlier in the discussion on knowledge, skills and abilities, the seminar leader should know the subject being discussed to the point that the use of notes should be minimal at best.

- *You need a considered plan for using media in support of your learning objectives.*

In itself, the use of media can visually enhance a presentation or discussion, but it is how media are used that will determine whether they add to or detract from the discussion, especially when students' attention is fixed entirely on these visuals, rather than on the leader. One should therefore exercise prudence when using visual and other forms of technology during a seminar meeting; a point that we will address again in greater detail in Chapter 7.

- *Be firm in maintaining the class schedule, but flexible regarding the revisiting of topics in response to student interest.*

The time allotted for each of your seminar sessions may be fixed and, as such, you may feel compelled to meet all of the goals outlined in your seminar syllabus. Indeed, both you and your students may expect that, by the end of each seminar period, you will have covered all of the topics assigned. Not doing so can be construed as poor management of time and/or discussion. However, this should not be the case, for two of the principle constructive presentation variables to which a seminar leader should adhere are those of flexibility and adaptability.

The seminar leader may find that the discussions have gone on longer than expected, yet they remain of great interest. There may be no resolution to what is being debated, or the scope of an issue may not be addressed to your satisfaction. You cannot hold the students longer than their scheduled time, since you need to be mindful of their schedules, as well as those of your fellow faculty members who may be affected if you run over your time limit. But the discussion should not be simply discontinued, for there may still remain learning opportunities to be mined by continuing the line of thought.

A useful approach to ending such a session would be to allow a speaker to complete his or her statement and then you, as leader, should halt discussion, inserting the caveat that it will be continued during the next meeting. The final points being made should be noted and those involved in the discussion at this point informed that they should be prepared to resume discussion at the next meeting.

One way to bring discussion to an effective halt with the intention of resuming the topic at the next meeting would be to say something like, 'Ralph's point is very well taken and it is clear that there is more to be said on this topic. I note, however, that we have reached the end of this session. What I would like to do at this point is ask you to hold onto your thoughts, as we will continue this discussion at our next meeting. I know that the syllabus has us going on to another topic next time, but I believe that, based on the discussion to this point, there is more to be said. Let us therefore pick up on this again first thing when we next meet.'

With such an approach, you, as seminar leader, are demonstrating not only the virtue of being flexible in terms of the seminar interests, but you are also adapting your course schedule to fit the needs of your participants. Such positive approaches to the conduct of the seminar may not have necessarily been expected by your students, but your willingness to be flexible and adaptable will almost certainly be appreciated.

If this approach to presenting is to be a hallmark of your seminar, then it may be best to inform participants of your intent, both in the syllabus and in your introductory comments during the first session.

• *Set the tone during the earliest stages of the seminar.*

The conduct of the seminar during the first two or three sessions will lay the groundwork for the remaining sessions. As we saw in Chapter 3, students will form lasting (and not always accurate) impressions from the first moments that they enter the seminar room and meet you. It is thus critical that these initial impressions formed by the students be positive, providing them with the motivation to stay with the seminar and play an active role in its conduct.

Therefore, ensure that your seminar participants know what to expect, both from you as their leader and the content requirements.

You should reinforce what was said during the first meeting briefly at the start of the second meeting. Let students see that you really wish them to be clear as to how the seminar is to be conducted during the meetings to come. Address their questions as thoroughly as possible, being certain that, with every answer, you add at the end, 'Did I answer your question?', or 'Did I clear up any confusion you may have had?' If the answer is 'yes', then proceed. If the answer is 'no', then ask the student, 'How can I best answer your question?' This provides the student with the opportunity to re-address his or her original concern such that it can be couched with better clarity or insight, helping you to better respond and the student to better understand. Doing so helps create closure to any remaining confusion a student may have.

- *Be prepared to deal with challenging students early on.*

No matter how much you attempt to guide your seminar, you will find that there will be one or more students who will provide you with various types of non-academic challenges. Some will appear bored or inattentive, while some will engage in inappropriate and disruptive conversation with other students. Still others may arrive at the seminar meeting late, or not at all. If graded assignments are to be submitted, some students may hand these in late without offering appropriate reasons. There may also be those students who, despite your encouragement, may be loath to participate actively in the discussions and therefore remain silent and passive.

These are but some of the challenges you may face. You must ask yourself how you should deal with each. The answers are as varied as the challenges, but each course of action should reflect the individuality of the particular student. Remember that, as a leader, you must ensure that all participants adhere to the seminar policies and requirements. You should use tact when addressing any problematic behaviour but, at the same time, remain firm. You may be able to resolve some of these challenges with a single discussion; however, you may find that, for those issues that cannot be resolved, further action on your part may become necessary. It is imperative that the seminar environment be constructive, precluding student behaviours that could become distracting and, ultimately, disruptive. Maintaining seminar cohesion is one of the paramount responsibilities of the seminar leader and your responses to issues that challenge this notion should be swift and decisive.

- *Be available for your students outside of seminar.*

One critical aspect of developing a positive bond with students is to ensure that they can contact you during those times that the seminar is not in session. Your students may wish to discuss issues that, for various reasons, could not be broached during the designated seminar period. Knowing that you are available to do so not only provides students with a sense of appreciation for your limited time, but also shows them that you are willing to meet their needs. Your willingness to take time and discuss issues with your students is a critical part of leading seminars and teaching, regardless of whether these exchanges occur during designated office hours or at impromptu meetings.

Addressing these basic points will provide a foundation on which you can continue to build your seminar with each subsequent meeting. However, having a foundation in place is just the first step to accomplish when creating a structure. There must also be strong walls and supports throughout, for without these the structure will surely collapse. In Chapter 5, we will examine one of the most critical of these supports: the creation of an environment of collaborative learning that encourages and rewards ongoing discussion and debate.

▶ Summary

In this chapter, we have seen that creating a positive learning cycle throughout the course of the seminar depends primarily on your ability to understand and employ those skills that can promote successful facilitation. These include setting realistic expectations for both yourself and your students within a framework of mutual respect and commitment to making the seminar a challenging and rewarding experience.

To further bolster the positive learning cycle, from the outset you should monitor, assess and, if necessary, refine your presentation skills. These are critical not only to impart and facilitate the exchange of information, but also to help direct challenging students to become active and constructive participants. You should also make it clear that the seminar bond does not break once the seminar meeting comes to a close. Rather, students should be made aware that you are available to meet with them during office hours, or at other mutually agreed times. In this way, you are helping to reinforce the seminar bond beyond the limited time devoted to the seminar meeting itself.

KEY CHAPTER TAKEAWAYS

▶ The positive cycle is a product of your planning and enthusiasm; prepare well and infuse your seminar with energy to ensure a swift start.

▶ If a serious problem arises early in the course, be prepared to intervene promptly. Left untreated, seminar problems tend to get worse over time.

▶ Remember the seminar leader–student covenant requires you to create an environment conducive to learning so that your students will want to fulfil their end of the bargain and contribute.

▶ Be accessible and approachable to your students.

5 Encourage discussion and collaborative learning

At this point, your seminar is well under way; you have led one or more sessions, but you are finding that the amount of discussion, especially among students, is less than you had hoped or anticipated. You have a couple of students who seem eager to raise their hands and engage in discussion, but the majority of your students appear reluctant to do so. You are concerned that such limited discussion as you have may even diminish further. What should you do at this point?

You will recall from our earlier discussion that the purpose of seminar-based instruction is not simply to 'transmit' information from the faculty to the seminar participants; that can be achieved through plenary lectures, or by providing handouts to participants. One of the key responsibilities that you, as seminar leader, will have throughout the entire course of each and every meeting is to promote an environment where collaborative learning takes place. Collaborative learning is characterized by an interactive approach to 'searching for understanding, solutions, or meanings, or creating a product'.[1]

To achieve this aim, the seminar discussion should involve all group participants actively interacting with each other (as well as with you as the leader) in what may be termed a 'discussion matrix' – a principle characteristic of a seminar whereby participants will direct their comments to others in the participant group, with one or more participants then responding, directing their comments back to the originator as well as to others in the group. The latter will then, in turn, respond and the matrix will (hopefully) expand to include the entire participant population.

Remember that it is all right – indeed, even desirable – for seminar participants to address one another directly during the seminar. What you lose momentarily in terms of control is more than compensated for by the value of direct interaction among your seminar participants.

It is, of course, your responsibility to provide guidance when these interactions lose steam or spin off into tangential topics.

This ideal state is not easy to achieve, especially since most students are used to other seminar discussions that may superficially resemble this type of interaction, but actually fall far short of achieving it. For example, all too often the seminar leader and a small minority of students will dominate the discussion, perhaps with these students directing comments to one another, but leaving the majority of students as bystanders. Even worse, some seminar instructors will provide one-way commentary directed at the group – in effect, turning the seminar room into a mini-lecture hall.

Less-experienced seminar leaders may feel more comfortable lecturing than guiding a class discussion. Or it may be easier to direct his or her attention toward those participants who appear attentive, responsive, even proactive in their discourse. The problem is that such discourse tends to be exclusive rather than inclusive, thus resulting in the remainder of participants feeling disconnected, disinterested, or outright bored by the discussion. A seminar leader whose participants are in this state will thereafter have a very difficult task in building (or re-building) the positive and self-sustaining cycle that is so critical to the success of a seminar.

Your primary means to create and maintain a successful collaborative learning seminar environment involves asking your participants thought-provoking questions that relate to the assigned learning objectives. This approach lends itself to students holding dialogue with one another, while you intervene selectively to inject new approaches to a thought, reinforce what one or more participants may have voiced, summarize what has been discussed to a certain point, and (due to time or topic constraints) re-direct the discussion in line with the lesson objectives. It all sounds rather straightforward. However, the reality is that it is not always easy to promote collaborative learning in the seminar room. Let us take a moment to examine four of the principle impediments to fostering collaborative learning.

▶ Impediments to generating discussion

The transmit–receive approach to education

Since their earliest years in school, most students throughout the Western world have been educated in the transmit–receive model; the teacher instructs and the student listens, at times questions, and then regurgitates in some way what has been 'learned'. The teacher then reinforces or corrects what the student has regurgitated and moves on to the next idea at hand. Conducted over a number of years, this particular type of classroom 'culture' is inculcated, integrated and eventually regarded as the norm. For seminar participants for whom the transmit–receive approach has been their principle culture in education, collaborative learning techniques and the Socratic Method may appear quite alien – and, perhaps, even unsettling. This could lead to participants being reticent, even averse, to the free and open expression of thoughts, even when urged to do so by seminar leaders.

The classroom authority gradient

In Chapter 3 we introduced the term 'classroom authority gradient', which helps explain why some students may be reluctant to engage in discussion with those whom they believe possess more expertise in an area. They assume that, because of a seminar leader's background, experience, age or a host of other less tangible measures that the leader naturally knows more than the students on particular topics and is thus better qualified to discuss said topics. The seminar leader may be regarded as unapproachable in this regard; someone to whom one must listen and from whom one must learn. To discuss, question, disagree with – or, even worse, challenge – this authority may seem to some participants as being daunting, a sign of arrogance, perhaps even foolish. In doing so, the student believes that he or she may run the risk of embarrassment, should the seminar leader – especially one lacking in social tact – heartily reproach the student in public for a comment or belief. The sad, yet predictable, result is that students are cowed into silence.

Stress and social insecurity

There are those seminar participants who, given their personality or lack of social skills, may be somewhat uncomfortable publicly expressing their opinions, or asking questions of instructors and/or other participants. Such reluctance to engage in discourse may be founded in unfortunate earlier experiences: a participant's own belief that he or she lacks the depth or quality of knowledge necessary to address a topic, the fear of being viewed by a seminar leader and/or other participants as being ill-prepared or even foolish, or even the debilitating effects of stress resulting from the sudden loss of comforting anonymity. When addressed directly by others – especially a seminar leader perceived to be intimidating – such participants may grasp for words, appear inconclusive or confused, provide inaccurate or incomplete thoughts or, in some cases, remain silent, clearly uncomfortable, hoping that the train of discussion and associated attention will be quickly (and mercifully) directed elsewhere. The result can be a breakdown in communications with such individuals, to the point that, should this state not be addressed by the seminar leader, these participants could conceivably remain silent for the remainder of the seminar.

Disinterest and complacency

It is not always clear what motivates students to attend a seminar. In some cases, it is purely the desire to learn in general, or reflects an interest in a specific topic. For some, it may be that they are required to attend the seminar in order to fulfil an educational programme requirement. In other cases, attending a seminar may be necessary for promotion, professional development, or a prerequisite for taking other courses of study. For some of these students, however (especially those who consider seminar attendance to be an unfortunate necessity), they will be there reluctantly and, as a result, may show little interest in what is transpiring. They may appear bored, ill at ease, aloof and disengaged, and may become complacent about fulfilling seminar requirements.

Students fail to complete assigned readings

As noted earlier, the readings provide your seminar with intellectual fuel for discussions. As such, they are critical to the success of your seminar. If the seminar contributions are lagging, you may suspect that the students are not doing the assigned readings. To confirm your hunch, you should ask very specific questions about the readings.

Example

In preparing for this class you read a provocative article about British heroines in nineteenth-century literature. What is the author's main thesis, and how well does she support it?

Example

The author of today's reading offers three competing explanations for the fall of communism in Russia. Who can briefly summarize these explanations for us?

Without such questions being asked, your students will quickly – and correctly – conclude that there are no immediate consequences for not doing the reading in the seminar itself. (Students who fail to complete the readings also put themselves at a disadvantage regarding written assignments.)

By asking reading-specific questions, you will immediately acquire a sense of whether the students are, in fact, doing the readings, ignoring them, or perhaps just undertaking them superficially. Praise is important. So, if the students are doing the readings, then you should encourage them to continue. If students are ignoring the readings, or are dealing with them superficially, you also need to address this issue immediately, reminding the students why you have selected certain readings and how they support the course objectives. You want to show them that the readings enrich the seminar discussions, making them more interesting and more substantive. You should also inform them that you will continue to ask reading-specific questions throughout the course. This approach should encourage most of your students to come prepared. Even taking these extra measures may fail to convince all your students to do the assigned readings. In these cases, individual counselling is recommended.

These, then, are but a few challenges to the creation of a collaborative learning environment in your seminar classroom. Know, however, that such challenges can be met and, through a host of interventions, be overcome. Let us explore some of these next.

▶ Techniques for creating and maintaining a collaborative learning-based seminar

Barrage technique

One variant of the Socratic Method discussed in Chapter 1 that is designed to stimulate collaborative learning is to pose a series of questions in rapid succession. This 'barrage' of open-ended questions is an approach commonly used as an introduction to a debate, a keynote address, or a panel discussion. It provides the 'audiences' of these events with a 'taste' of what is to come and some of the areas to be examined. As such, it provides a menu previewing what is to appear on the dinner table.

The seminar leader can also use the barrage technique as a point from which to launch into discussion.

Example

The discussion during our last meeting and our assigned readings for today raised many interesting and thought-provoking questions. You may recall that George (indicating one of the participants in the group) had some very strong opinions about the impacts of globalization on Asian economic stability. With that in mind, there are several questions that we will consider today. These include the following: Do you agree or disagree with George's main argument about globalization? Has globalization impacted world economies? If so, how? If not, why not? How is globalization affecting international trade, if at all? And has globalization made it easier or harder for states to exercise autonomy over trading practices and ethics?

This rapid fire questioning technique is not meant to confuse; rather, by placing several questions on the table you are, in effect, giving seminar participants the opportunity to pick and choose which to answer. It may be that a participant is not able to recall what George said last week, but may indeed have some opinions about whether or not globalization has had impacts on national economies. If George's earlier statements were the heart of the current discussion – the only question asked, then a participant not knowing or recalling what George said would effectively be shut out of discourse on this topic. That participant would remain silent, detracting rather than contributing to the seminar. However, when several questions are posed to participants at the outset, the fact that a participant may have forgotten George's earlier arguments no longer serves as an impediment to participation. Rather, participants who may be struggling with the material can pick and choose questions that they are most comfortable addressing.

The seminar leader employing the barrage technique should do so with care. It is possible that, when faced with a series of questions, a participant may become overwhelmed, even intimidated into silence. You can preclude this, however, by reassuring students along the following lines:

Now, none of you is expected to have the answers to all, or even some, of these questions. However, I encourage you all to feel free to contribute to the discussion, providing us with your general thoughts about one or more of these issues. By the way, as always, I remind you that debate is encouraged, so don't be afraid to question or challenge one or more of your colleagues here – that is what this seminar is all about.

With such a statement, the seminar leader has not only given participants leave to participate in the discussion to the best of their abilities, but also to engage one or more of their peers in debate. The leader will guide the discussion and debate to ensure that not only does the discourse stay on topic, but also is conducted in a civil manner.

Using questions to create a discussion 'weave'

The discussion 'weave' is one of the most important and powerful seminar techniques. You, as seminar leader, use the discussion matrix to summarize a number of differing yet salient points made by several participants. From these many points, you can then pose to participants a further single question that moves the discussion to a higher level of complexity and nuance.

For example, after a given period of discussion involving several participants talking about the use of medical tests on animals for the purpose of developing medicines for human beings, you could say something along these lines:

We just heard from Henry, Victor and Sophie about their views on the use of such animal testing. Henry believes such research is critical, since it helps to predict effects on humans without risking human lives to do so. Victor thinks the use of animal testing may be necessary, but only under a set of strict conditions agreed to by the international scientific community. Sophie thinks it can never be justified under any circumstances. What do the rest of you think? And what does international law have to say about the use of testing in such research?

As this example illustrates, the weave technique creates many opportunities to reiterate key points and move the discussion forward. It generates insights and connections that may otherwise go unnoticed.

The weave provides a tapestry of insight and nuance that ties together seemingly distant or disconnected points in an intelligible whole. The weave also allows you, at least potentially, to engage all your seminar participants in a guided discussion. It reinforces the importance of accountability, since participants know that their faculty member has listened to, and remembered, their remarks.

A well-run discussion weave increases the chances that your seminar students will engage in real dialogue, as opposed to serial monologues. The distinction here is crucial. The former is conducive to learning; the latter, polemical posturing.

The discussion weave is essential to collaborative learning. But remember that not every conversational thread will be relevant. It is your task to discern those threads that are relevant from those that are irrelevant – and to weave the relevant threads into the discussion accordingly. The discussion weave will help you to reference key learning points and to move the group beyond other points that may not be particularly relevant to the discussion. To this end, you can list key points on the blackboard, computer screen, flip chart, or whatever visual medium you prefer to use to reinforce learning.

Well, what do YOU think, Professor?

At some point in your seminar, perhaps very early in the course, one or more participants may ask what you think about a particular issue. Recall that your role as seminar leader is to lead, guide and facilitate. By soliciting your thoughts about an issue, you are being asked, in essence, to become an active participant as well. But is this something you really wish to do? Indeed, your experience is such that your thoughts and opinions contribute to facilitating a broader exchange of views, and encourage students to participate – even on some rather sensitive issues. However, it is possible that, by stating your own views, you may inadvertently be inserting some biases into the discourse, and thus dissuade some participation that otherwise may occur.

There are some students who, recognizing your role as an authority and subject matter expert, may be loath to express views that could contradict yours. This harkens back to the classroom authority gradient (p. 33). The result could be that some students may fail to state their own views or beliefs openly for fear of being disrespectful, for fear of public humiliation should you rebuke their views, or for fear that expressing contrary or differing views will necessarily impact their seminar grades.

If you believe that your personal contributions to discussions can benefit the seminar in some way, then it is critical that you lay the groundwork for doing so in such a way that your comments will not be perceived as unassailable. There are several ways to set the stage for your comments. Prior to presenting your personal thoughts, you should preface your comments with a sentence or two, noting that the views you express are, indeed, personal; that they do not reflect the opinions of the institution or organization that employs you. You are, in essence, for the duration of your personal remarks, suspending your state as a representative of an organization or institution.

Such use of 'disclaimers' are commonly observed at professional conferences where a presenter (especially one representing a government body) wishes an audience to know that the work to be presented cannot be attributable to the organization where he or she is employed; neither can the organization be thereafter necessarily held accountable for the speaker's comments. Of course, the reality here is that, regardless of such disclaimers, one often cannot simply shed one's identity or accountability, especially when a heresy can lead to one being dismissed from that organization or institution. However, in a truly neutral academic setting where differing opinions are welcomed, discussed and openly debated, it should be possible to exchange such diverse views within civil discourse.

The question remains, however, should you as the seminar leader do so? If even after providing a disclaimer you remain uncertain of this answer, then you could also consider the following:

- It would be helpful here to take a moment or two to describe the classroom authority gradient and some of the ways that it may impair free and open discussion. As such, make certain that your students understand the differences between your established role as seminar leader and your added role as participant. Let them know that your views may be based on your personal experience, but that you remain open to all views, especially those that may not be in concert with your own. Remind students that their opinions, whatever they may be, are important – even critical – to the success of the seminar.
- Assure participants that their comments will never be held, or in any way used, against them, either during discourse, or when their grades for the seminar are prepared. Remind them also of the 'non-attribution' policy (pp. 39–40) as it is applies to the seminar.

- Of course, you can always turn around the 'What do you think, Professor' question by asking, 'That's a great question. What do you think?' or, 'What do the rest of you think?' However, this type of question reversal approach should be used judiciously, lest the seminar participants conclude that you are evading their queries.

In general, then, it is not inappropriate to provide your own personal contributions to a discussion. However, in so doing, do not forget that the roles you don as a seminar leader cannot simply be discarded as a participant, and that some of your students may not (at least, at first) be comfortable engaging you directly, especially when their comments or opinions may differ from yours. Still, if you employ some of the tips provided, you may find that your students may engage with you in discussion and even lively debate and, by including you, strengthen the positive cycle of discourse.

Employing humility

One way to minimize the classroom authority gradient is to exhibit a sense of humility. This does not necessitate your becoming self-deprecating; rather, the notion of humility as it is used here is as a method designed to remind your students that, even though a subject matter expert, you are far from omniscient.

Now, for some instructors the idea that they may be perceived by their students as anything but infallible would be not only disconcerting, but a totally unacceptable situation, a disgrace resulting in a loss of face and credibility. For such individuals for whom esteem is critical, the discomfort from not being able to address a question could manifest itself in several ways. For example, the instructor may exhibit the same behaviours as would a participant experiencing a similar situation; that is, be at a loss for words, appear uncertain, or stumble through a rather transparent response that is less than adequate.

Alternatively, the instructor may create a facade of confidence, assuming that what is provided as a response will naturally be accepted as gospel by students. The nature of such responses may not be entirely relevant to the discussion but, when couched with a demeanour of self-assuredness, it is likely that students may be convinced that a satisfactory answer has been provided. Such responses by a leader may be more accurately referred to as 'winging it' or, in more current political terms, 'spinning'. In using such an approach, the instructor may, in a misguided way, take self-satisfaction that he or she managed to survive an otherwise embarrassing situation by appearing to answer a question successfully and without a loss of credibility.

The dangers in this approach, however, are many. 'Winging' and 'spinning' can be viewed by students and colleagues as fraudulent means to an end, placing the ego-based comfort of the instructor above the needs of the students. The instructor continues to run the risk of damaged credibility, especially if a student is later, in public, able to contradict the 'winged' answer. Further, using such an approach in the first place may be an indicator that other, even more 'destructive' approaches are being employed during the conduct of the seminar.

How, then, to avoid the pitfalls of 'winging' and 'spinning'? Exercising humility is one answer. If asked a question that, for whatever reason, you are required to answer immediately, then it is acceptable – indeed, ethically imperative – that you acknowledge this. You can do this without bringing embarrassment to yourself or to those who asked the question.

Example:

Susi, you have asked a great question about the origins of Stonehenge. I do not know the answer. Let me do some research on this and get back to you shortly.

It is as simple as that. You have not only admitted that you do not have the entire knowledge of the universe at your immediate disposal, but that you will take the time and effort needed to find an answer (if one is available) and then provide the questioner with a response. You can do this either by personal correspondence with the student or, even better, at the start the next seminar meeting, addressing all of the participants with an opening akin to the following:

You may recall that during our last meeting, Susi asked me about the origins of Stonehenge. I've done some research on that question since then and believe I have an answer for you, Susi. I'd also like to know what the rest of you think about this.

By providing a response in this manner, you have not only answered the particular question with authority and credibility based on a foundation of research but, in doing so (and especially by asking for their own thoughts), you have also included the entire participant group, thereby building further on the positive learning cycle you seek to promote for your seminar.

Another option would be to ask the question of the entire class to see what their replies may be. Doing so would stimulate open discussion between the students in which you, as seminar leader, may wish to participate or not. In the end, if you believe that Susi's question has not been adequately answered, you can always note that you will address this question at the start of the next seminar meeting. This will provide you with some time to research the question further.

What if, during the course of discussion or debate, one or more of your students points out an error on your part? You should regard this as a victory, not humiliation, for in feeling sufficiently comfortable to the point that he or she could freely challenge something that you have said, you have, by the use of constructive facilitation skills and strategies, helped that student truly to embrace the sense of seminar – something that they may have never been afforded in the past. Thus, if you have imparted incorrect or incomplete information, know that it is always best to admit this immediately, thanking the student(s) for bringing the error to your attention, noting that their doing so was the correct course of action to take. Using such a humility-based approach will strengthen the 'bond' with participants by 'allowing' them openly to exercise their intellectual freedom to question. While this outcome may not be appropriate in all situations, it is certainly one that you must engender for your seminar to be successful.

Reasoning by analogy

In the absence of historical knowledge, seminar participants will tend to reason by analogy. Here, you must ensure that participants are aware of the various strengths and weaknesses of using a particular analogy. They should be reminded that, while analogies are helpful tools for better understanding a topic, analogies by definition seldom provide exact parallels. Despite this, if handled with care, further analysis of such analogies can provide many teachable moments for the participants.

Example

Some commentators have compared economic problems in the European Union with those of the United States? Is this analogy valid? How are the situations similar? How are they different?

Referencing current events

By selectively referencing current events, you will highlight the relevance of the course material to the real world. That said, you must also be careful not to allow your seminar to become too much of a current events seminar, since such discussions tend to be impressionistic and superficial.

Example

Last week we discussed the role of the media in conflict situations. How would you characterize the role the mainstream media is playing in the recent uprisings in the Middle East?

Turn to your neighbour technique

Another useful technique to stimulate discussion and critical thinking is the 'turn to your neighbour' approach. This technique provides participants with the opportunity to engage with one another in a manner that, up to that point, they may not have been doing. It forces the less-active participants to become involved and, at the same time, helps reinforce the participant bond that you have been striving to maintain.[2]

Example

Take a minute and write down a list of three reasons why reforming secondary education is so challenging. Then turn to your neighbour and discuss how and why your reasons are similar or different.

After giving the participants a few minutes to discuss such a question or topic with their neighbour, you should reconvene the seminar and compare the results among the group as a whole. It would be unwise to permit these discussions with neighbours to continue for extended periods, since doing so may result in the students discussing subjects not necessarily relevant to the topic at hand.

For this technique to work smoothly, you may need to make some temporary changes to your seminar seating plan. If possible, pair off a usually less-responsive student with one who you know has been active during seminar meetings. Try to create pairs where students differ from one another; that is, students from different cultures, having different native languages, experiences, major areas of study, and so on. This technique can be particularly effective early in the course, since it can also function as a means to 'break the ice' between students who may otherwise be reticent to meet one another.

The team or working group approach

If the number of participants is sufficiently large, you may consider dividing them into teams or working groups, and then asking each group to address a specific topic. At a subsequent, regularly scheduled meeting of all seminar participants, you would then lead them in a discussion of the issue, asking that a representative of each team present the team's responses to the assignment. In doing so, you are again reinforcing collaborative learning while providing students with a creative means to express opinions. Using this approach, teams would be provided with times to meet and discuss whatever issue(s) you have assigned.

You may wish to create your teams or working groups using a random selection process of some type, or by employing a purposeful approach whereby you create groups based on your particular needs or purposes. Teams or working groups should not be large; the larger the group, the more unwieldy it may become. Indeed, it has long been recognized that the most effective working groups are usually limited to between five and eight individuals[3] and, when complex problem-solving is required, such groups should optimally be even smaller.[4]

Further, less-responsive participants can retain their quiet 'anonymity' when in large groups – something that is not possible when they are part of smaller groups. For instance, in a seminar of 30 students, you may wish to create six groups of five members each, while in a seminar of 15 students, you may wish to have three groups of five participants each.

Research has shown that role-playing is an important component of inquiry-based learning.[5] Seminar leaders might wish to employ the various roles described by Dr Lois Hart in her book

Faultless Facilitation (1996), whereby every member of a working group is assigned a role with specific responsibilities. These roles typically include that of the group leader, recorder, and devil's advocate, among others. This approach ensures that all members of the group are actively involved in its discussions and required activities.[6]

Your selection of the group 'leader' is critical; this is the individual who will ensure that the group adheres to the requirements of the 'assignment' or requirements you may provide. That 'leader' should be a student who you know to be an active participant, one who you believe can effectively guide the team toward its goals. It would therefore be helpful, once again, not only to review the biographies of each of your students, but also to take into consideration those interactions you may have already had with them during seminar meetings. The remainder of the group roles should be assigned by group members themselves.

Ensure that there are spaces available – either within the seminar room or outside – where these groups can meet. The group leader or members could select a venue of their choice, or you could assign a particular location as desired.

There are several ways to employ this team/working group approach:

Within-group

Each team can tackle a given issue or question from a within-group perspective, whereby members of the group will discuss issues or questions in an attempt to reach some goal or set of goals. For example, you may instruct your groups to answer the following question: 'Do you believe it wise to use military forces to tackle civil security issues like domestic policing?' The teams or groups would then discuss the issue and, depending on whether or not your instructions required team responses to reflect a consensus or not, arrive at a single response that would be discussed subsequently with the entire participant group.

Between-groups

In this form of discourse, teams or working groups would be assigned opposing roles to be engaged in subsequent debate. Each group should be required to come to some consensus regarding a particular issue, and then be prepared to debate that issue defending the perspective to which they were assigned. A spokesman assigned for each group by its leader will represent the group's views during ensuing debate and/or discussion. You should instruct the group that dissenting opinions will be respected and that the group leader has an obligation to report such dissent.

In pursuing this between-group approach, the seminar leader must be conscious of the fact that there will be those participants who may find that taking a certain approach associated with specific sensitive issues may be very difficult. The assignments for the groups to consider should, therefore, be couched in such a way so as to best avoid issues that may result in participant alienation.

Once-around-the-seminar-room technique

This technique can be very effective to get everyone involved in the seminar, and it is simple to execute. As the term implies, you proceed around seminar room and ask participants to ask the same (hopefully interesting) question. This approach can yield some revealing contrasts. But be advised that this technique is time-consuming. Even if each participant gives a relatively short answer, it will still take considerable time to hear from everyone, so plan accordingly.

Finally, if you use this technique more than once, be sure to alter your start points, since seminar participants who go early will have less time to reflect on their potential contributions than those who follow them. If you used the technique going around the seminar in a clockwise fashion, then next time you should reverse the order and proceed in a counter-clockwise fashion.

The role-reversal technique

Asking seminar participants to adopt and argue a perspective contrary to their own biases is another powerful tool in the seminar room. The biases of your participants will become clear within the first few seminars. The role-reversal technique forces the participant to consider a different, perhaps even opposing, point of view. The key is your ability to set up a scenario that will stretch the participants' imagination and understanding of complex issues.

Example

For John, who is a career diplomat:

John, let's imagine that you now are the senior military officer in a small Central European state. Your armed forces are suffering from old equipment and poor morale. What reforms would you seek to enact to ensure your armed forces will be capable of executing their assigned missions?

Example

For Melinda, who is a career military officer:

Melinda, let's say you are now the Foreign Minister of a South Central European state that has recently suffered a spate of terrorist attacks. What actions may you consider with your neighbours to improve your border security?

Using silence as a tool

Most seminar leaders will consider silence during a seminar problematic – the result of many of the challenges to collaborative learning discussed earlier in this chapter. While this may be the case, silence also can be used as a powerful tool to stimulate discussion and to reinforce or emphasize certain points.

As instructors, most of us are uncomfortable with silence, especially when it follows a question we may have asked our students. We vainly scan the group, looking for signs of understanding and impending response, and become somewhat disconcerted when none follows. Is this silence because the students did not understand the question? Are they bored, or generally uninterested? Does the question address a very sensitive topic, making the students uncomfortable and therefore loath to present their views?

Although you may be pondering these questions during this glaring period of silence, you may also consider the lack of response as being a time for potential respondents to give thoughtful consideration to an answer prior to its execution. Giving students these moments of silence can thereby become an acceptable – and, in some cases, even desirable – means to stimulate conversation.

It is therefore recommended that, when asking students for their opinions, comments or answers to questions, you should allow for silences. Just wait a few moments until someone ventures forth a comment. At first, this may feel quite awkward, especially when such silences seem to drag on for longer than the period of your own tolerance. However, in many cases, students will be similarly uncomfortable. You may even tell the group that the seminar cannot proceed until an answer has been provided.

While somewhat heavy-handed, this tactic will eventually yield a response. However, the rule of thumb here is that, once you or a participant asks a question or requests an opinion, you (and the questioner) should not say anything until another participant ventures a comment or an observation. If you become impatient or overly uncomfortable with the silence and you do end up saying something before your participants do, then this technique loses its force and credibility.

▶ Providing seminar summaries

The use of seminar summaries is a simple yet effective means to challenge students and, in doing so, keep them interested and involved. Some seminar participants may, on occasion, express their frustration with the Socratic Method. To some, the novelty of being in an environment based on intellectual give-and-take will be stressful. For others, your seminars may seem like an endless series of questions and frustrating intellectual puzzles.

Your ability to provide a brief summary at the end of each seminar can help assuage these concerns. The summary does not need to be lengthy or detailed. In fact, distilling key discussion points linked with the learning objectives for the particular class should only take a couple of minutes. This is your golden opportunity to drive home key points related to the learning objectives.

In formulating the summary, the emphasis should always be on the participant contributions. What did they learn and discover through the course of discussion? Providing a summary can help bring the discussion to closure. It can also provide a stepping stone to the next seminar. Also, remember that providing a 'summary' is not the same as providing 'closure' on issues. After all, most complex issues defy simple or facile answers, and some key issues and themes will recur throughout the course.

Example

Today, we discussed the tension between security measures and civil liberties, which you will recall is one of our learning objectives for today. Several of you provided examples of how this tension can result in civil liberties being compromised in the name of security. Other seminar participants noted that civil liberties will never gain traction, let alone flourish, unless there is some semblance of order and security in the first place. Please keep these potential trade-offs in mind. We will return to this issue next week when we discuss international terrorism in greater depth.

Example

Please keep in mind our discussion today regarding ongoing research at the Large Hadron Collider in Switzerland. You noted that, although costly, research conducted at this facility has been vital in finding some critical answers to the most puzzling mysteries of particle physics. Several of you also emphasized how cutbacks in spending by other countries could impact important research like this being conducted around the world. Later in the course you will be called upon to make specific decisions and trade-offs in one of our exercises.

As your seminar participants gain confidence, you may want to call upon one of the participants to provide a summary of the discussion. You should begin by asking one of your more talented participants to provide a model for the seminar. You can help by providing some advance warning to the designated participant, so that he or she is not caught by surprise.

On the other hand, if you have a strong seminar group overall, you may not want to provide any advance warning. This approach may encourage a higher level of attentiveness from all your seminar participants, since they will not know who will be designated until you identify the person at the end of the seminar.

▶ Field studies

Another way to stimulate discussion and collaborative learning would be to take them 'on the road' to engage in 'field studies'; that is, excursions to venues outside of those where seminar meetings are usually conducted. This approach provides another robust dimension to inquiry-based learning.

Conducting seminar field studies: benefits and costs

Benefits

▶ Contact with resources not available at usual seminar venue

▶ Direct first-hand exposure 'brings to life' previous learning based solely on media

▶ Allows for the conduct of activities not possible at usual venue

▶ Changes learning environment.

Costs

▶ Can be expensive and time-consuming

▶ Logistical support can become unwieldy, especially for a large seminar group

▶ May necessitate special scheduling; conflicts could preclude some students from attending.

As the sidebar shows, there are several benefits and costs to taking seminar students on field studies. Of all these, the principal reason for conducting field studies is to provide students with an array of resources that may not otherwise be available to them (and you) at the usual seminar venue. These resources can vary in nature and scope.

For example, if your seminar topic on a particular meeting day concerns air traffic controller workload, you may be able to present this topic using readings and videos. However, would it not enhance the discussion to take your students to an air traffic control centre to meet controllers and hear their thoughts on their work responsibilities first-hand? It may be possible to bring these controllers to your usual seminar venue, but it is only at the air traffic control centre itself that students can experience for themselves the operational environment. Such exposure can only add to the depth of understanding of the topic at hand and thus greatly contribute to the quality of discussion.

Another important benefit of field studies is that they can 'bring to life' whatever is being discussed. Students rely on gathering information and holding discussions based on what they see and hear within the usual seminar venue. You may be highlighting certain ideas through the use of mixed media applications. However, essentially, you are relying on the student's ability to learn about – and, perhaps, vicariously experience – an event; to construct a reality that, ultimately, may or may not be accurate. Field studies provide another dimension of learning whereby students can add first-hand experience to their developing understanding.

Here is another example. At the George C. Marshall European Center for International Security, where both authors have taught seminars, terrorism is a frequent topic of discussion. The terrorist attack on Israeli athletes during the 1972 Olympic Games in Munich, Germany, often comes up in this context. The vast majority of students attending the Marshall Center have learned about this incident through various forms of media. This is not surprising, since there are a host of resources available to those who wish to learn about this event. However, Marshall Center seminar leaders routinely take their students to the place where this incident occurred to better understand what transpired and how such a tragedy could have come to pass.

Students are taken to the athletes' housing area at the Olympic Village in Munich so they can see the apartment where terrorists held some athletes captive. Students are able to see the balcony of the apartment where a balaclava-clad terrorist stood, peering down. To this point, most of the students had only seen the now iconic photograph capturing this moment for posterity. Now, at the Olympic Village, they are able to look up at the very same balcony; the image in the mind's eye is made real. They can also see the surrounding structures and, doing so, can better understand the complexities associated with the handling of this incident.

The field study visit to the Olympic Village invariably enlivens seminar discussions held on site – which demonstrates, among other things, that the Socratic Method is not limited to the classroom.

To take another example, if a seminar leader wishes to discuss American Civil War encampments, doing so in the classroom would be limited to employing media and perhaps a guest speaker or two. However, there are various Civil War societies located throughout the United States that routinely conduct realistic re-enactments of Civil War battles. Members of these groups have devoted a great deal of time, effort and study to the history of those who actually took part in the hostilities and their daily activities, part of which being the accurate re-creation of battlefield encampments.

A field trip to meet in the field with members of such a group – to see them in their nineteenth-century uniforms, to watch them as they engage in activities associated with daily life in these encampments – greatly adds to the student's understanding of the topic at hand. Students are able to watch the re-enactors, observe their behaviours, listen to conversations between soldiers as they may have taken place, smell the odours of cooking and get a sense of the close-quarters, less-than-sanitary living that prevailed more than a century ago. Clearly, it would not be possible to conduct such a demonstration in the seminar room.

Finally, there is the notion that students may simply enjoy the change of scene. Taking them away from the usual seminar venue could change the context in which a subject is being discussed. Some students may feel more comfortable discussing certain issues away from the usual venue and its particular environmental setting. Typically, field trips help with the seminar bonding that occurs when students share a new experience. The enhanced seminar bonding, in turn, can help energize seminar discussions to the extent that students feel more comfortable with one another, and with you, as the instructor.

Most students will find any alteration to a fixed routine stimulating. By participating in a field study that may involve travel to another venue and at a time other than that usually associated with a seminar meeting, it takes students away from perceived regimentation, introducing them to some variability in their daily schedules and activities. It is possible that this introduction of novelty could result in some changes in their behaviour. Indeed, there is some evidence suggesting that novelty-seeking behaviour (neophilia) can lead to increased levels of creativity[7] – which is something that you, as seminar leader, should be striving to achieve.

As noted earlier, there are also some costs to conducting a field study that, in the course of your planning, must be considered when deciding whether or not to engage in such an activity. One of the major limitations to being able to conduct field studies is the cost of such endeavours. If your field study requires you to travel some distance away from your regular seminar venue, then you may have to find ways to transport your students to the venue. Commercial transport (including chartered vehicles) can, at times, prove to be expensive. Arranging for meals and (if necessary) lodging for students and faculty, as well as providing payments to your off-site hosts, can similarly further tax already limited fiscal resources. You must ensure that, if you wish to incorporate field studies into your syllabus, you have a reliable funding source to support these endeavours.

Another cost incurred is that of time. While it may be possible to conduct a field study during a regularly scheduled seminar meeting, it is more often the case that field studies require more of your time and that of your students. If you and your students are on schedules requiring you to engage in activities prior to and subsequent to your seminar meeting, then it may become necessary to plan for such activities to take place at the end of a daily academic schedule. In some cases, field studies may require that you and your students be absent from the usual venue for an extended period of time. This would require the juggling of schedules and possibly extensive communications with a number of other individuals who must account for and/or approve such undertakings.

As well as there being fiscal and time costs, the logistical arrangements for such field trips can become fairly complex, especially when your seminar student group is large. Can you transport your group from your venue to another in a safe and effective manner? Have you arranged for representatives at the destination to meet your group and provide assistance? How will students be able to accommodate schedule changes and other work-related requirements that may be impacted by the field trip? Is there an itinerary or plan established that addresses the conduct and goals of the field trip? These are but some of the logistical challenges that must be addressed prior to departure. It is strongly recommended that you, or whoever oversees these logistical responsibilities, have them completed and approved well before the start of the field study.

As noted, field studies of durations longer than that available during regular scheduled seminar meetings may have to take place during hours that may conflict with other student responsibilities (attending other courses, employment, other non-seminar related activities, and so on). There is a risk that such schedule conflicts could preclude the possibility of a student participating in the field study. Careful field study planning and coordination with others impacted by a student's participation could help resolve any such conflicts. However, if more than one activity is affected by a student's absence, resolution could become more difficult.

▶ Summary

One of the greatest imperatives – and, at the same time, challenges – facing a seminar leader is the fostering of creative, constructive and ongoing discourse. By doing so, the successful seminar leader is able to create and maintain a state of collaborative learning during the entire course of the seminar. In this chapter, we have not only examined the impediments that could prevent your seminar from being truly collaborative, we have also described a number of facilitation techniques that, if effectively employed, will help ensure the creation of a positive learning cycle based in a collaborative learning environment.

KEY CHAPTER TAKEAWAYS

► Challenge your students in creative and constructive ways to help to keep them engaged throughout the semester and to maximize learning opportunities.

► Varying your techniques will help encourage discussion. Over-reliance on any one technique will prove counterproductive.

► The 'discussion weave' is one of the most powerful techniques to promote seminar-based learning. It promotes collaborative learning by engaging students with the Socratic Method and requiring them to evaluate multiple points of view.

► Making your students provide a short summary at the end of the seminar will help them develop a valuable skill and give you a strong sense of how well they are absorbing the material.

► Field study trips are another excellent means by which to challenge your students. They are encouraged to the extent that time and cost considerations allow.

6 Team teaching challenges

Team teaching involves the use of two (or more) faculty members leading a seminar group. Team teaching in the context of inquiry-based learning can be especially rewarding for students and educators alike, but it also presents challenges which require careful preparation to overcome.

Sometimes junior faculty will be paired with more senior faculty members. In these circumstances, it is clear who has the lead for the planning and execution of the seminar. In other cases, faculty members may well be equivalent in seniority and experience, so the question of who leads at what point requires resolution.

If you are assigned to co-teach, then it is essential that you sit down at the earliest possible opportunity to coordinate a reasonable division of labour for the course. This division of labour should cover everything from who drafts the syllabus to who has the lead for individual classes. The sooner you develop a common understanding of the division of labour with your teaching partner, the better.

You may be tempted to think that co-teaching may cut your preparation in half, but it seldom works out this way. The advance coordination required for a successful seminar actually increases the workload of both instructors, in some respects.

There are, of course, many different ways to divide up the course when it comes to co-teaching preparation. One approach may be to set up the course so that you alternate leading individual class sessions on a weekly basis. Another approach may be to divide the course as a whole into two parts, with each instructor taking the lead on their respective halves. Or the division of labour may be less symmetrical. For instance, you may be the seminar lead for the first three or four meetings. You may then hand-off your role as lead to a colleague for one, two or more meetings, after which you would return to your principle lead role.

It is imperative that you ensure that those faculty to whom you are handing-off the leadership role are aware of the issues discussed in this book (you may wish to provide them with a copy prior to their doing so). If you apply the principles of inquiry-based learning during your classes and your teaching partner decides that he or she simply wants to lecture in seminar, then you have a real problem on your hands. As you can see from the sidebar below, for students there are both benefits and costs to using the hand-off approach.

Benefits: With team teaching students become exposed to various types and styles of facilitation. Although they may have the same goals in mind for a seminar meeting, faculty members can vary greatly in the way they address groups. Assuming that both faculty members are working within the general parameters of inquiry-based learning, this may prove a refreshing change for students and will help re-energize any waning attention.

Students benefit from a wide variety of faculty experience. It may be that if your syllabus incorporates discussion on a topic or topics with which you are not very familiar, you may find it better for you and your students to hand-off the seminar to faculty who are subject matter experts on a particular topic. Doing so would bring to bear that faculty member's years of experience into the discussion, making it more relevant, accurate, timely, in-depth and thought-provoking.

Costs: Students will naturally begin to compare and contrast seminar leaders over a host of qualities and characteristics, not all of which will necessarily be relevant in terms of teaching effectiveness. The problem here is that such impromptu assessments (fair or not) could potentially impact students' willingness to participate, or the manner and depth of their participation during subsequent seminar meetings where you or another faculty member may be leading. You may address this issue when telling students that there will be some seminar lead hand-offs during coming meetings, noting why this is being done and how it would be less than constructive to use faculty comparisons to govern the nature and scope of their participation.

Not all faculty may be as acquainted as you are (or soon will be once you finish reading the handbook) with the challenges to leading a successful seminar and the strategies to overcome these challenges. The result may be that the faculty member to whom you handed off the leadership role may use one or more 'destructive' leadership approaches, as discussed earlier in the text. This could prove detrimental to, and even undermine, the foundation and support strategies that you had already put into place (and that were working!). It is therefore imperative that you have complete confidence in the leadership skills of the faculty member to whom you wish to hand-off the seminar.

It is possible that, for some students, a change of seminar leadership could prove disconcerting. They may have become comfortable with your style and approach to leadership, making them more amenable to active participation. However, should a different leader appear, it may take some time for the student to feel as willing to participate actively.

Team teaching: student benefits and costs

Benefits

▶ Students are exposed to various types and styles of facilitation

▶ Students benefit from a wide variety of faculty experience

▶ Subject matter experts are better able to address topic-specific questions falling outside your expertise

▶ Speaker variety helps to garner and hold attention

Costs

▶ Students may unfairly compare and contrast seminar leaders

▶ A less-skilled, hands-off faculty member may use 'destructive' leadership approaches that could undermine the positive learning cycle you had already created

▶ Change of leadership could prove disconcerting to some students

---

There are also several benefits and costs for seminar leaders when using the team-teaching approach. Whether for a few intermittent meetings or an extended block of time, being able to hand-off the leadership of the seminar can provide you with an invaluable opportunity to take stock of the course. During the time away from being seminar leader, you could review, and even revise, your notes for future meetings. You could also spend some time on other professional activities, the results of which could have some bearing on your seminar. Stepping away from the seminar leader role would also allow you to become a course observer.

As an observer, you would be able to see how (or whether) your students interact with the other faculty member(s), noting some of the constructive and destructive faculty–student dynamics taking place. You could subsequently discuss these dynamics with your colleague. In doing so, you can better exchange ideas about the course and better coordinate approaches to presenting and discussing topics. Such collaboration can also manifest itself as improvements to course materials, and provide critical insights as to the nature and scope of the content and delivery.

Another cost to handing-off the seminar leader role is that if you are not physically present at each meeting, you may find that you have lost track of what has transpired. You may become unaware of possible changes in course dynamics, seminar bonding issues, as well as the content and pace of discussions. This loss of situational awareness may result in your being 'out-of-the-loop' and unfamiliar with the state of the seminar.[1] During the next hand-off back to you, such a loss of situational awareness can impede your ability to make a swift and smooth transition back to the role of seminar leader, the result being a change in the dynamics between you and your students. The way to prevent this from happening is to ensure that you and your team-teaching colleague(s) meet frequently to discuss the state of the seminar and any issues or problems with course content or the students that may have been identified. Doing so can provide a consistent team approach to resolving such issues.

Team teaching: seminar leader benefits and costs

Benefits

▶ Great opportunity to have subject matter experts work with students

▶ Provides you with a chance to observe faculty–student dynamics

▶ Provides time for further preparation of future meetings

Costs

▶ If you are unable to be present at the seminar, your being out of the loop could lead to unfamiliarity with seminar dynamics and progress

▶ Inability to answer questions or address issues discussed by colleague

▶ Could make the formation and maintenance of seminar bonding difficult

▶ Counselling students

You also need, jointly, to create procedures with respect to coun-selling students about their academic performance during the course. Communication is critical in this regard; you must keep each other informed regarding all substantive interactions with the students in order to avoid confusion and conflicts. You should agree to consult with each other before counselling individual students so that they do not receive mixed messages about paper assignments, requests for extensions, preliminary feedback on the seminar, or other academic topics. Also, you should avoid the possibility that a student may try to play one tutor off against the other. This infre-quent, yet unfortunate, occurrence is entirely preventable provided both seminar leaders are communicating with one another.

▶ Guest speakers

Guest speakers are, in effect, a variation of the team-teaching approach. The difference is that the other teacher is from outside your educational institution, and typically only used once during the course. Inviting guest speakers can stimulate and maintain interest and participation in the seminar. Doing so provides the same benefits and incurs the same costs as one finds when using the faculty hands-off approach.

Guest speakers from outside your organization may provide unique insights into topic areas that those from within cannot. For example, if your seminar topic involves art restoration and preserva-tion in Italy, you may wish to invite the director of a college or insti-tute of art conservation to discuss this topic. Or, if your seminar addresses the uses of technology in modern farming practices, you may invite the head of the local Agricultural Commission to discuss the controversy regarding the use of genetically modified seeds. In both examples, you have leaders in their respective fields bringing their unique knowledge and experiences to your seminar.

It may be possible for you to invite notable speakers, those in the public eye and in great demand for their expertise, to address your students. If that is the case, you may wish to open the seminar, or have a special expanded session where the guest speaker will address broader and larger groups of individuals associated with your organization.

Example

You addressing your students:

As you can see from the syllabus, we are scheduled next week to discuss European efforts to promote future space exploration. To help us understand this, I have invited Jean-Jacques Dordain, the Director General of the European Space Agency, to brief us on this topic. He will also lead us in a discussion on what you believe to be the appropriateness of these plans, and will be happy to answer any questions that you may have. Because of the great interest I expect this lecture to generate, I will be opening the seminar to the entire Department. You can thus expect a number of faculty and students not associated with our seminar to attend that day.

Ordinarily, guest speakers will not attend seminars for the sole purpose of leading a discussion. Rather, they will usually make a presentation for your students, the length of which should be determined based on the duration of your meeting that day. In this regard, you should plan for there to be time for post-lecture discussion and questions. Unfortunately, guest speakers are notorious for taking more time than allotted with their presentations, so take this into account when you discuss the desired length of the presentation. For example, if you really want your guest to speak for no more than 30 minutes, you should probably ask for a maximum of 15 or 20. This is necessary to avoid the frustrating, yet all too common, result of running out of time while students still have many unanswered questions for their guest speaker.

You should consult your organization's instructions on dealing with issues associated with guest speaker logistics, funding and transportation. Prior to the start of their presentation, your guest speakers should be informed of the 'non-attribution' policy (as described in Chapter 3) whereby discussions will be treated as privileged information. You should also make an announcement to this effect at the opening of the seminar meeting, drawing this to the attention of not only your own students, but also any other students who may be attending the session.

▶ Summary

In this chapter, we examined the dynamics associated with team teaching. If done well, team teaching can provide your students with academic richness and depth. If done poorly, team teaching can result in confusion and frustration. Advance preparation is essential. It will help create a rapport among the team, clarify the division of labour, and get the seminar off to a strong start. To sustain positive momentum, both team members must commit to close coordination and constant communication throughout the entire course.

This chapter also discussed how best to integrate guest speakers into your course. They, too, can add richness and variety to your class, but there are risks involved. With experience you will develop a sense of what topics best lend themselves to guest speakers. If you have a guest speaker who performs poorly this should not discourage you from inviting others if you believe they would add value to your seminar. Not every guest speaker will dazzle your students, but if you select them carefully and clearly convey the educational objectives you would like them to address, then most of the time things will work out well.

KEY CHAPTER TAKEAWAYS

▶ Team teaching involves a series of trade-offs. The advantages and disadvantages to team teaching require careful consideration in the preparation and execution of this approach.

▶ Team teaching requires constant communication to ensure a true 'team approach'.

▶ Integrating guest speakers into your course can greatly enhance your seminar by bringing in unique perspectives and providing your students with a change of pace.

7 Technology and seminar-based learning

The following three scenarios range from using no technology at all to employing internet and interactive slide tools. The question you must ask yourself, however, is which of these options accomplishes your seminar goals in the way you consider to be the most effective.

Scenario 1: You are leading a seminar on the histories of William Shakespeare and wish to illustrate your notion that Richard III was not really the tyrant the playwright portrayed. Despite the fact that you are not a trained actor, you recite a few key lines from the play. Your students sit quietly, watching and listening to you politely. You are concerned that your powers of oration may not be the best and you may have to explain in some detail what you have just read aloud.

Scenario 2: You are leading a seminar on the histories of William Shakespeare and wish to illustrate your notion that Richard III was not really the tyrant that Shakespeare portrayed. Realizing that Sir Lawrence Olivier's performance is a classic, you elect to show a video where Olivier recites some key lines from the play. The students sit quietly, watching the video until it ends. Olivier's performance is stunning and makes clear the meaning of the narrative you wish to discuss.

Scenario 3: You are leading a seminar on the histories of William Shakespeare and wish to illustrate your notion that Richard III was not really the tyrant that Shakespeare portrayed. Realizing that Sir Lawrence Olivier's performance is a classic, you elect to show a video where Olivier recites some key lines from the play. Using a laptop computer, you project a recording posted on an internet video website. You simultaneously project slides showing the narrative itself moving in synchrony with the video. You also use the computer to highlight certain lines of the narrative so as to draw your students' attention to their particular relevance. Further, you will have recorded the session on your course website page, enabling students to revisit what was presented and discussed as often and whenever they may wish – thus reinforcing learning by creating an environment of 'on-demand' information availability. Using an online 'chat' feature, students can then contact you or other students by email or the website itself, making comments, showing the particular slides or portions of the video about which they may have questions. You also provide your students with web-based links to scholarly works and media commentary regarding Richard III. Finally, you provide an online survey with which your students are able to provide you with comments relating to the particular session during which this topic was discussed.

To decide which option best accomplishes your goals, let us consider the costs and benefits of each of these approaches.

In scenario 1, where no technology is used, a clear benefit is that there are no technology or equipment costs required; you read the narrative aloud to students. Of course, one of the costs to this approach is that you may not possess the performance skills necessary to impart the meaning or intent of the lines of poetry you are reading. The result could be confusion on the part of the listeners as to the meaning of the narrative and your intent on presenting it. This could lead to boredom and non-participation.

Scenario 2 requires the use of basic technology: a video player of some sort, a projector and audio equipment. While this would require the purchase and maintenance of this equipment, you would be able to show your students Sir Lawrence delivering the lines with great style and eloquence. If you wish to make comments or highlight certain lines during the playing of the narrative, you would have to stop the recording, speak your piece and then re-start the recording from where you left off. As such, you would be disturbing the flow of the narrative – a characteristic that can be critical in poetry. It would also prove somewhat awkward, as you would be dividing your student's attention between the recording and yourself.

Scenario 3 provides you with the ability to play the recording without interruption while concurrently being able to interact with the narrative in real-time, without having to start or stop it. Using the computer and applications described in the scenario, students are able to watch the video, follow the narrative and watch for particular comments that you may provide. Students can interact online with you and other students. In terms of fiscal costs, you would need a computer with the desired application programs and a projector.

Clearly, scenario 3 offers the most complete and flexible approach of the three options. Not only are you able to present Shakespeare's work in a manner that will hold your students' attention, but also the technologies can help to provide more concurrent and interactive 'layers' of information that can stimulate conversation, both during the seminar period and subsequently. The online links and survey add to the interactive experience between you and the students, further reinforcing the seminar bond and maintenance of the positive learning cycle.

However, there is some risk associated with the use of technology of any kind. It is possible that your computer hardware or software may cease to function correctly, or at all. There is the possibility that you could lose your internet connection with the video website. You may discover that the desired video is no longer available on the internet, or, instead of Shakespeare, your clicking of the computer mouse could result in a different and undesirable video being projected.

With this in mind, let us turn to exploring a couple of the major questions you may have with regard to technology in the seminar: Should I use technology at all? If so, what types of technology should I employ? In answering these questions, it is important at this juncture to note that this chapter will not recommend or endorse any specific technologies. Any recommendation along these lines is likely to be quickly outdated. Instead, this chapter will provide some practical recommendations for when to use technology and the types that would best suit the seminar at hand.

▶ Should I use technology at all?

Your use of technology should help further inquiry-based learning. There is a body of evidence supporting the notion that 'the classroom environment becomes less teacher-directed and more learner-centred' when instructors use technology.[1] Despite this, you may still be wondering whether or not you should employ technology in your seminar.

The answer to this may be somewhat out of your hands, for the use of technologies in support of learning today is often the rule, rather than the exception. Indeed, it is rare that one encounters a learning environment wherein various technologies are not employed, both by instructors and students. Almost all students own, or have access to, some type of personal electronic device that provides them with the means to take notes, access resources, communicate and record. As we have already seen in earlier chapters, in order to ensure that a seminar is student-centred (i.e. designed for, and meeting the needs of, students), a seminar leader is obliged to provide students with an environment that facilitates learning. Noting that those attending a seminar are not there to be entertained but, rather, enlightened, the key is to use technology as a tool in support of the discourse.

In considering whether to use technology, it is useful to ask whether your students can achieve their learning objectives without using any technology. As we saw in Scenario 1, a seminar on Shakespeare's tragedies could consist of purely of readings and discussions; nothing other than the printed word on the page and your reading would be necessary in such a case.

However, as noted in Scenario 2, even if the use of technology is not critical, it can still be useful to enhance the learning experience, and should be used to do so, provided the costs and risks are manageable.

For example, if you were to use one or more of the media-based seminar support tools (films and videos, audio recordings, photos, and so on), doing so would require the implementation of various technologies. To show films and videos, one requires the use of a media player, amplifiers, loudspeakers and (if video) a projector. If the media or related information resources you wish to use are available only through access to the internet, you will require a computer configured to receive such information. In this regard (and staying with Shakespeare for the moment), may it not help stimulate discussion if, rather than you or a student reading from, say, Hamlet, you used an historic audio or video recording of the same text spoken by a great orator or actor? Which form of presentation may best serve your students?

If you wish your students to pursue some research prior to the next seminar meeting, you can either provide each with hard copy materials (a time-consuming and possibly costly enterprise), or recommend they go to a library to consult specific texts or journals (a problem when they are competing with others for the same limited resources). However, you could also ask your students to conduct web-based research in order to access a larger and wider variety of global resources within a very short time.

To keep your seminar student-centred, you should also consider recording your seminar meetings and making them available for later use by students who either could not attend a particular seminar meeting, or who wish to revisit a particular meeting. To do so, you will not only require the technology to make and store the recordings, but your students will also require the technologies that would permit them to access the recordings wherever and whenever they wish ('on-demand').

As we will see in the next section, there are a host of technologies that help to guide and drive student participation in unique and creative ways.

▶ What types of technologies should I use?

If you decide to use technologies in your seminar, what types should you use that would be best-suited for your students? With so many types of hardware and software available (and more entering the market every day), it can become overwhelming when having to decide how to use the various technologies available and what types would best suit the seminar at hand.

Media

When employed judiciously, the use of various media forms can effectively stimulate discussion, while holding the attention of your students through the use of photographs, films, videos and audio recordings.

Using multiple forms of media

While there are some seminar leaders and speakers who can enthral listeners with content quality and presentation style alone, the reality is that most of us rely on some types of media support, not only to take the place of the content, but to facilitate students' understanding. We will discuss the use in seminars of various media-related technologies in Chapter 8. However, for the present, suffice it to say that attention can better be maintained by illustrating what is being said through the use of various types of media (i.e., slides, videos, other types of projections, graphics, recordings, artwork, and so on).

You have probably seen paintings from the earlier days of medical education where a physician and his students are standing about an operating table. A dissection on a deceased human is taking place, with the physician not only describing the anatomy of a particular organ, but actually showing the students those portions of the organ to which he is referring. Actually seeing the organ may facilitate the understanding (and possibly also the retention) of what is being concurrently said.

If your seminar is, for example, discussing Allied and Axis national leadership during World War II, it may be helpful to project photographs or show videos of these leaders while you or your students are making a point. You may also wish to have a number of mixed media sources available in order to help bring resolution to a disagreement. For instance, a student may state that the German Army (*Wehrmacht*) massacred hundreds of Polish officers in the forest of Katyn. As a function of pre-meeting research, you may have access (perhaps by means of the internet) to documents with conclusive evidence showing that it was the Soviet Army that had carried out that massacre. You could project copies of those documents, or even play a recording of an elderly survivor of the Katyn incident describing what actually occurred.

It is important not to use these mixed media tools to rebuke what a student is saying. We have already seen that such direct public rebuke can prove destructive to the positive learning cycle.

Example

You, addressing the particular student giving erroneous statement:

Gabe, your statement is not based on evidence and is therefore incorrect. As you can see from this page from the document 'Investigation into the Katyn Massacre' dated 1987, it was the Soviet and not the German Army that was responsible.

The student who erred may only glance at the projected image, refusing to examine it or anything else that follows given his or her embarrassment. However, if you couch your response to the erroneous information in such a way as to be non-punitive, it is likely that the student that has voiced the incorrect statement will not be embarrassed but, rather, will have learned from the media-supported evidence.

Example

You, to all seminar students:

It is a common belief that the German Army carried out the Katyn forest massacre. This belief is based on evidence provided by Kremlin

*investigators in 1945. However, there is evidence uncovered since
then that suggests that the Soviet story may not be accurate;
indeed, this latest evidence suggests that it was the Soviet Army that
carried out the Katyn massacre. As we know, history can be
somewhat fickle, so we can expect that, as evidence is uncovered, we
will have to contend with possible revisions of what we thought,
until that point, were facts. Many thanks to you, Gabe, for helping
us make this very important point!*

Thus, by presenting the media-based evidence along with a tactful explanation, you have reinforced the constructive learning environment without estranging one or more of your students.

Films and videos are especially successful not only in 'grabbing' students' attention, but also in providing the grist for discussion. If, for example, you are exploring the impacts of propaganda on public persuasion, you may wish to show a film or video representative of this genre. This would be followed by discussion.

After showing the seminar group a video of the 1938 Sergei Eisenstein film *Alexander Nevsky*, you could open up discussion to the group: 'Well, having seen the film, what do you think about it? Was it a good film? What about the film as an instrument of Communist propaganda: how effective was it? What messages do you think it conveyed to Soviet viewers? How (if at all) did Serge Prokofiev's soundtrack impact what you were seeing?'

In this way, the video becomes the stimulus for discussion and debate. At this point, you may also wish to further illustrate your discussion with examples of propaganda couched in various other media forms: literary (you can pass around books or pamphlets), artistic (you can project photos of artwork used for propaganda), verbal (you can play audio recordings of speeches) and visual (you can show other propaganda films or videos).

The presentation of these various media forms requires the use of different in-class technologies, including projectors, media players, amplification equipment and loudspeakers. Depending on the resources provided by the venue where the seminar is being conducted, these assets may be readily available. However, this may not always be the case. Attempting to locate, furnish and set up this equipment immediately prior to your seminar meeting can be fraught with difficulties.

As noted in Chapter 2 on seminar preparation, it is highly recommended that well in advance of the first session of your seminar, you should ensure that not only are the technologies that you will require are available, but also that you have access to local, experienced, on-call technical support should it become necessary.

The importance of having timely and reliable technical support cannot be stressed sufficiently. Whether associated with the operation and maintenance of media devices or any number of computer-based technologies, the trained information technology (IT) specialist assigned to your academic department is probably the most critical of all your seminar assets. It is strongly recommended that you become well-acquainted with the IT specialist(s) with whom you will be working during the course of your seminar. Make them aware of when and where you will be conducting the seminar and the technology-related needs that may exist. Doing so will help them understand your requirements, thereby enhancing their ability to serve you and your students.

Computers

Whether a large personal computer (with separate tower, keyboard and screen), or a smaller one-piece portable system incorporating all of these elements, computers present the seminar leader with a vast array of capabilities for information creation, gathering, storage and presentation. Along with the many types of computers available, there are a great number and variety of seminar-supporting software 'tools' that can either be purchased or be available without cost. The software that is designed and used to deliver educational content online is known as a learning management system (LMS) (also known as a virtual learning environment, or VLE). Instructors can use these systems to post announcements, courseware, assignments and feedback for their students. Students can use these platforms to deliver their assignments, to blog, and to form discussion groups.[2] Depending on their level of sophistication, these platforms may also come equipped with a variety of additional tools, as indicated in the sidebar.

Learning management tools for computer-based seminar support

- ▶ Presentation design software

- ▶ Programs that create and enhance collaborative learning

- ▶ Research tools (including statistical packages, citation searches, and so on)

▶ Hardware and software that allows playing of online video recordings

▶ Software that facilitates creation of audio-visual slideshows

▶ Hardware and software that permits user to create and listen to audio files

▶ Hardware and software that permits user to create and listen to video files

▶ Software that facilitates organization of files (slideshows, video and audio files, and so on)

▶ Software that converts audio and video from one format into others

▶ Software that enables the creation and maintenance of webpages.[3]

As you can see from the sidebar, the list of learning management tools is quite extensive. Within each of these classes falls a wide variety of LMS-related software programs that, if properly used, have the potential to enhance the learning experience of your students.

The 'if properly used' caveat merits close scrutiny. With the many benefits of using these tools come inevitable costs. Besides the fiscal and technical resources necessary to acquire these tools and subsequently install and use them, there is the potential to become overly-dependent on these tools.

For example, a number of software firms have developed programs by which users can create slides that can be projected using a computer and hardware and or web-based data storage resources. In addition to the visual presentation provided by each slide, the presentation creator can embed additional audio and visual files within a given slide. So, for example, if a given slide was describing the surface of Mars in a written narrative, the creator of the presentation could (with the appropriate action) activate a video or audio file that would be presented concurrently with that particular slide. Further, with the selection of various links on the slide itself, the creator of the presentation can redirect the serial path of the presentation to another slide or information source that may, or may not, have been included in the original presentation. Such are the remarkable advantages offered by computer hardware and software.

However, having this array of capabilities so easily available can be a siren's lure, leading the presentation creator into over-dependence on such devices, resulting in overly-complex presentations that rely more on entertainment than on quality of content. As such, the direction of the discussion could shift away from the speaker and onto the presentation media. Such a distraction can only impair the development and maintenance of the positive learning cycle you are seeking to create with your seminar.

Indicators that your use of technology has crossed the line from education to entertainment:

▶ Your seminar students are unduly focused on the technological medium, rather than the substance of what you want to convey.

▶ The technological medium evokes a powerful emotional response among your students at the expense of intellectual discourse.

▶ Your seminar students seem to crave a technological high that derives from your over-reliance on eye-catching audio-visual tools.

Student response applications

During the course of discussion, you may wish to poll or quiz your students regarding a particular topic. One commonly will verbalize a query, asking for responses. In such cases, a handful of students may respond, while the rest remain passive. As such, only a portion of the seminar group is represented and the responses may be less than satisfactory. There are, however, technologies available that, when combined with LMS (VLE) software, can provide seminar leaders with a more concise and representative sampling of data from students.[4]

Students are able to respond actively to questions with an element of choice (including multiple option, true–false, no–yes, and so on) using hardware (e.g., pushing a button, activating a switch, or even inputting data and text) that is electronically interfaced with computer programs that are able to note how many participants actually provided an answer, to tabulate the inputs, and to provide a statistical analysis of the inputs. Such devices (sometimes referred to as 'clickers' or 'polling devices') are small, lightweight and can be designed to perform a number of interactive functions. All of this is accomplished automatically and the results can be seen within seconds.

Although it is assumed possible that such software can provide the identity of students who failed to respond or who responded incorrectly, using such a system (especially where anonymity is guaranteed) may make students more prone to take an active role. They may be more likely to push a button or activate a 'clicker' than to voice an opinion or provide an answer with which they can be associated (a problem made even more negative if the answer is incorrect).

Seminar leaders who use this technology must do so with care, especially when it comes to formulating thought-provoking questions. Equally important, instructors must take care to ensure that the use of clickers does not result in a game show atmosphere, which is inconsistent with an educational environment.

The internet

While the stand-alone computer may be all that you require for your seminar, you should also recognize that connecting the computer to the internet will provide you and your students with the ability almost instantaneously to access a global host of audio, visual and document-based resources, many of which would be otherwise unavailable.

Guidelines for student use

Most universities and colleges today have policies on the use of personal electronic devices by students. If so, you need to familiarize yourself with such policy and make sure your students are aware of it. If not, then you need to articulate some commonsense rules for student use of electronic devices in your seminar. Failing this, there is a high risk that your students will be distracted by their electronic devices during the course of the seminar.

> **Guidelines for student use of electronic computing and communications devices in the seminar room**
>
> ▶ Use of electronic computing and communications devices during a seminar is restricted to seminar-specific requirements provided by the instructor.
>
> ▶ Students will not 'surf' the internet, text or email during the seminar.
>
> ▶ Students will silence alarms, ringtones, and any other noises that may distract the seminar leader or their fellow students.

There are several tools associated with the internet that you can harness to help ensure the success of your seminar.

Using emails to communicate with students

The advent of electronically transmitted mail (email) started a revolution in the way we communicate. No longer is it necessary to account for the time and distance between correspondents; emails, text, audio and visual messages can now (using various types of devices) be sent digitally to almost anywhere in the world at speeds limited only by the quality and connectivity capabilities of local network or internet email hosts.

As it is very rare today that a student will not have access to some type of electronic mail system, it is highly recommended that you use email to keep in contact with your students. This mode of communication has several advantages.

Consider email as a time-saving tool. You wish to send a message to the entire seminar group. Rather than having to send the message out to each student individually, you can create a group email address that includes all your students and, with one press of a button, send your message out simultaneously to them all.

Email also allows for ongoing contact: Your seminar group may meet only once each week. However, you may wish to forward them information, answer questions or otherwise maintain contact with your students in between seminar meetings. Email provides an effective and efficient way of doing so.

One or more of your students may not be able to attend a particular seminar meeting. You can use email to correspond with them about the missed session, noting any special points that were discussed, relaying important information or providing a means for these students to comment and ask you questions. This type of communication becomes especially critical if, for some reason, a student is not able to attend several seminar meetings.

You can address time-sensitive issues. There will be occasions when students may have comments, concerns or questions that must be addressed immediately; some issues cannot wait until the next seminar meeting. You may not always be available by telephone. Thus, your students should be assured that they can contact you with these issues via email. In turn, you should routinely check your email several times each day to ensure that you are aware of any time-sensitive issues that must be addressed, and so that you can respond to such queries in a timely manner.

On this point, it is important that you set reasonable expectations regarding your response time. Your students need to know that you have other responsibilities beyond their particular seminar, which means you may not be able to respond immediately to their queries. Thus, you should convey your anticipated response time (whatever the case may be), noting that circumstances will dictate how quickly you will be able to respond.

While the vast majority of students today have access to email, occasionally you may encounter a student who has never used a computer or personal electronic communications device and therefore lacks a person email account. As email correspondence plays a critical role in your seminar, it is therefore recommended that the seminar description (provided to all potential students prior to the first meeting) includes the requirement that students have some means by which to access a personal email account.

Creating a seminar website

All resources on the internet are created, manipulated and stored on web-based pages located on a website. Webpages, in essence, are workbenches on which information is created, manipulated and stored. Depending on the security setting you select, access to a website (and all or some of its pages) may be open to all others using the internet, to specific individuals, or to a select group of internet users.

As almost all of your students will have a computer or some other communications device that can connect to the internet, it is strongly recommended that you create a website devoted to your seminar and publish it for use by your students. How your seminar webpages are created and published will depend on the preferences of the organization that you represent, or by which you may be employed. In many cases, the college, university, government body, corporation or organization with which you are associated may require that you first receive approval to create a seminar website, provide you or an information technologist with the format and tools with which to create the website, and then have it published as part of their own 'umbrella' website.

For instance, if you are a professor at a university, you may work closely with their IT specialists, providing them with all the information you wish to display on your website. They can then help you design the look of the site (possibly adapting it to an already standardized format), and ensure that the capabilities you wish to include are there and functioning. The IT specialists would then provide you with all of the support you may require to update the website, and solve any problems that you and or your students may encounter while accessing the site.

Websites are splendid tools that can be used in any number of ways. For example, you may wish to use your seminar website as a central location to store all of the resources your students will require during the course of the seminar. These can be attached as files that can be accessed through links to internal (local computer-based) and or external (web-based) information sources. Such resources can include audio, visual and documented copies of various presentations, discussions, demonstrations and supporting information.

Your seminar website can also serve as an excellent platform to provide your students with information. Creating a webpage Seminar Leader 'Announcements' section in which you can provide text messages will help your students to obtain information you wish to impart in a timely and effective manner. In this regard, it would be best to remind your students to check the seminar webpage at least once daily for any information you may provide in the announcements box.

The webpage can also be used as a seminar chat room wherein students can provide recorded or text messages to you and/or others attending the seminar. For example, one of your students may have a question or comment about an assignment. There should be a function associated with the chat box design that allows whomever wishes to use it to select the recipient(s) of a given chat (i.e., you, another student, several individuals, the entire seminar group, and so on). In cases where more than one specific individual is selected as the chat message recipient, asking a question using the chat box will result in responses not only from you, but also from other students. The chat box is thus another useful tool with which students can interact, cooperate and collaborate with one another.

If your seminar syllabus requires that students complete assignments (and most do), the website you create can prove to be a perfect central location to which students can submit their assignments. You can create a webpage within the site specifically designated for assignments and therein provide the means for students to download their assignment files (that they more than likely created using their own computers) to that page. You can then access that page at your leisure, open the files and review what was provided by your students. If the assignments are to be graded, you may wish to include a separate secure webpage-based capability to provide your students with their grades and assignment feedback.

Social media

Web-based communications have expanded dramatically in recent years through the use of various types of social media. These internet-based platforms are designed to provide for the quick and effective exchange of various forms of information between individuals and groups with the intent of promoting social interactions and interactive collaboration. As one analyst summarized, 'social-media technologies, such as social networking, wikis and blogs, enable collaboration on a much grander scale and support tapping the power of the collective in ways previously unachievable.'[5]

It can be debated as to whether or not the exchange of information using such social networking sites can help you and your students meet their educational objectives for the seminar. Remember that the nature of your seminar is for ongoing instruction at a level that can prove quite different from that of less formal social discourse. However, your students may elect to create a seminar-related social media site. Such use of social media could prove yet another effective means of fostering collaborative efforts in support of the seminar. It should be noted, however, that with email and a seminar-specific webpage already in use for such purposes, your students may decide that the added use of social media could prove distracting, confusing and, ultimately, unwarranted.

Confronting obsolescence

One of the greatest challenges you will face when using technologies of various types is that of obsolescence. It is almost a corporate imperative that, as soon as a brand new product becomes available, the design, development and production of its successor should already be well underway. This notion can be especially applied to the various technologies discussed in this chapter.

An unending barrage of advertisements trumpet the sales of new personal electronic devices that are more powerful and compact than ever – all claiming to perform more quickly and efficiently than the very device that you purchased (at great cost, no doubt) but a short few months ago. You may, at times, even find that your students are using devices far more sophisticated than those that you have available for your seminar.

The seminar leader must therefore ensure that there is compatibility between the technologies he or she is using and those being commonly used by students. This can be achieved by requiring either that the venue hosting your seminar have the most up-to-date technologies available to you, or that your students possess technologies compatible with yours.

With regard to the first option, you will have to see how any limited fiscal resources that may be available can be used to upgrade or replace ageing technologies. This can be a massive challenge in an organization where you may be competing with others for these resources.

In terms of the latter option, you should make it clear to students prior to the start of the first seminar session that they will require computers or personal communications devices that can access the internet-based resources that you may be providing. In reality, you will probably find yourself using both options. However, it is more likely that the second will prevail, as many of the newer technologies remain compatible with those that, although but a few years old, will nevertheless be thought of as obsolete.

▶ Summary

In this chapter, we have seen that there are a host of basic and advanced technologies available to you as a seminar leader that, when used effectively, can greatly support your ability to carry out a successful seminar. In today's environment, where technology, internet-based information exchange and social media may drive needs (rather than vice versa), it is possible that you may find yourself becoming quite challenged to learn about and use technologies of which you have little experience or understanding. This can be a positive state of affairs; by being able to incorporate the use of these technologies into your seminar effectively, you are better meeting the needs of your students at their level of technological prowess and, in doing so, helping to ensure that the goals and outcomes of your seminar will be met.

KEY CHAPTER TAKEAWAYS

► Using technology for the sake of technology serves no educational purpose. If properly used, technology can promote inquiry-based learning.

► Instructors must ensure technology is used for educational purposes, not entertainment.

► Technology should help promote your learning objectives, not vice versa.

► If you are going to use technology in the classroom, then you must rehearse its use to reduce the potential for distracting technological problems during the seminar.

► Technological glitches can and will occur, even with rehearsals. Think through potential problems and remedies before they happen.

8 Distance learning

As we have seen throughout this book, the basic 'structure' of a seminar involves a group of students gathering at a single venue where, under the guidance of a seminar leader, ideas are exchanged in verbal discourse. In the past, those wishing to attend and actively participate in a seminar must have been physically present at the seminar venue to do so. Not so anymore.

The internet and its tools developed over the past few decades have made the in-person requirement obsolete. Those who, for a host of reasons (distance from the seminar venue, time or fiscal limitations, and so on), may not previously have been able to attend a seminar are able to do so now using internet-based distance learning (DL) (also known as 'web-based' or 'e-learning') technologies. Indeed, it has long been recognized that one of the greatest advantages of being online with the internet is its great ability to promote and facilitate DL-based collaborative learning.[1] DL has proven immensely popular; so much so that there are now a host of universities and other institutions that have committed themselves to providing quality education and training by means of DL. The educational venue changes with DL, but the core dynamics of inquiry and questioning remain. The inquiry-based learning approach to higher education thus applies well to DL.

The extraordinary growth of DL in recent years has significant implications for you, as a seminar leader. Simply stated, seminar leaders who limit their exposure to DL will find their professional opportunities progressively more limited in the future. Technology has opened wide the doors of the seminar room to participants from around the globe, providing them with previously unavailable educational opportunities.

How does DL work in practice? One way is for seminar students to connect via their own electronic resources to a central server that houses the seminar website that you have constructed. What this does is permit access to your webpages not only by your students who are physically present, but also by those students attending the seminar from afar.

You may concurrently provide a means for your students to 'attend' the seminar either 'live' (i.e., as it is happening in real-time) or in recorded form. There are several ways to accomplish this.

You can broadcast the seminar meeting via streaming, whereby the audio and (if you desire) video feeds are directly transmitted via the internet to the DL student. If your seminar is being streamed and does not employ any visual media and you do not wish DL students to see (or be seen by) other students, then you may wish to provide an audio-only format for your meetings. This format requires that you have a microphone or several microphones staged in positions that can clearly pick up voice inputs (yours included). Similarly, as your intent is to have an interactive seminar, the audio-only format requires that your DL students have a microphone (either stand-alone or built into their computers) with which they can provide vocal inputs.

An advantage of an audio-only format is that it does not require the use of a great deal of internet bandwidth, thereby somewhat lowering the possibility of delayed or distorted internet transmission during streaming. A disadvantage of an audio-only format is that it precludes the DL student from having any access to visual elements that may be used in the seminar venue. This could result in a loss of situational awareness whereby the DL student may not be able to understand what is being described without the aid of the visual support being provided to students physically present in the seminar room. The result could lead to some confusion about the topic at hand and possibly a withdrawal from active participation.

The approach taken in this book is that successful seminars are characterized by the prudent and effective use of both audio and visual media content. DL students should be presented with all of the same audio and visual elements as those presented to their *in situ* counterparts.

To accomplish this, you can employ an interactive web conferencing program that provides for any number of students from afar to simultaneously link-in to a live seminar. Such programs allow DL students to hear (via microphone) and see (via video camera) what is transpiring and, at the same time, provide them with real-time interactive capabilities. If they have a microphone, they can address the seminar group through speech. If they have a video camera, the seminar group can see the DL student. If neither microphone nor camera is available, the DL student can participate via a live chat box, similar to that found on your seminar website. As such, you and all of your students can interact and collaborate using these technologies.

Seminar meetings conducted using these programs can usually be recorded and played back on demand.

These programs also incorporate the capability to show DL students visual resources associated with the brief – the same that are being presented to those students located on-site in the seminar room. This is best accomplished by transmitting digitized real-time images (photos, graphics, slides, videos, and so on) to the screen being viewed by the DL student. It is therefore recommended that as many of your audio and visual resources as possible be digitized and transferred to computer-based files that can then be shown simultaneously to both in-situ and DL students.

Finally, most of these interactive programs also provide the capability for real-time chat between the seminar leader and students, as well as between students. As noted earlier, the use of chat can prove effective in stimulating communication should any students be reluctant to do so verbally.

▶ Advantages of distance learning

Clearly, by employing DL technologies, those conducting a seminar will be able to reach a large, worldwide group of participants who would have otherwise not been able to benefit from the seminar. The opportunities to expand the knowledge-base as well as to incorporate discussions from participants representing a host of countries and cultures have the potential to stimulate and broaden the conversation at hand.

Another advantage is that such DL seminars can be available at a relatively lower cost for students living and working far from the location of the course. Attending by means of DL technologies precludes the need to locate funding for travel, food, lodging and other daily expenses that one would incur when attending a course in person. The affordability of DL thus permits students to attend the seminar; without the technology, they would not otherwise be able to do so.

Students who may not have the mobility or access to attend educational opportunities in person due to various medical issues or disabilities are able to attend courses without having to travel or go to a location from which the course is conducted. DL technologies and modern computer interfaces have been designed to promote such access. For instance, an individual who lacks manual dexterity is able to employ voice-interactive technology to operate computer hardware and software. For those without mobility, a computer equipped with DL-related software can be brought to them.

Students who are already involved in their careers can tailor their daily schedules to attend a DL seminar. Many employers today not only accommodate such requests to do so, but actually encourage their employees to take DL courses that will further enrich their professional backgrounds (thus making them even more valuable and productive employees). Schedule flexibility becomes even more important for these individuals that have families and other personal responsibilities.

▶ Disadvantages of distance learning

As we saw in Chapter 4, physical proximity and movement (the very things you are not afforded with DL) play major roles in the conduct of a successful seminar. With regard to DL students, you, as the seminar leader, lose the ability to exercise these critical elements in seminar leadership when you are not able to be physically close to the participants, to see their faces and note their body language, to move about the venue, thereby requiring your students to follow you visually, to confront students spontaneously (especially those not very actively engaged) by placing yourself next to students and directing a question specifically to them (or, in turn, listening to what they have to say). With DL, you may or may not even see the face of a student; you may simply hear a disembodied voice, which is something that could, at first, prove somewhat disconcerting for some leaders and students. However, it is likely that it would not take long for the DL student to feel like, and be regarded by others as, a member of the seminar group.

Another disadvantage to DL seminar conduct is associated with one of the risks of using the technology described earlier; it is possible that, during the course of a seminar meeting, the hardware or software used by the seminar leader or the DL student may fail. Depending on the age and quality of the technology used, such failures could be rare or frequent. It is also possible that there may, for any number of reasons, be internet host/server technical disruptions in the transmission of the seminar. Should that occur, the signal between the DL student and seminar computer would be lost. Such losses of signal can be quite brief (some web conferencing programs can respond and automatically reconnect lost signals within seconds) or, if the problem is major, last for a much longer period. Although the DL student could later play the recorded version of the seminar discussion, doing so would be less desirable than having the opportunity to contribute directly in the real-time discourse.

Another disadvantage may be inherent in the format and use of the technology itself. As noted earlier, there are students from various cultures who may have had little contact with the Socratic Method of discourse, and whose societies may even discourage its use. Still others may not possess the sophistication and technical prowess to use (or learn to use) the technologies associated with taking a DL course. Both cultural and technological variables could help build behavioural barriers that would cause some to not contribute to the discussion, or to not remain with a DL seminar, even if they were otherwise assisted in doing so.

Ultimately, it will be up to you and course/curriculum planners to weigh the costs and benefits of including DL students in your seminar. If you believe that your seminar can benefit from the inclusion of DL students, then it may be best to inquire as to whether or not the venue can support such an effort. If, on the other hand, you believe that the costs of having one or more DL students as part of the seminar outweigh the advantages, then it would be best to limit your student population to those who can attend in person.

▶ Blended seminars

One very popular approach to education that brings together the uses of various types of media and technologies with DL is the notion of conducting a course by employing what is known as 'blended learning'. According to the Macmillan Dictionary, blended learning can be defined as 'a method of learning which uses a combination of different resources, especially a mixture of classroom sessions and online learning materials'.[2] Such materials (or media) can take various forms, including information stored on a computer, some form of digital media, or on a distant internet server or 'cloud'. The concept of blended learning is founded on the notion that, by effectively combining (creating a fusion of) face-to-face meetings and technology-based resources, students should be able to become (and feel) actively (cognitively) engaged in the learning experience.[3]

Blended seminars can involve the use of synchronous (i.e., the conduct of a seminar in 'real-time') as well as asynchronous (whereby the student can obtain learning materials on demand, but at the cost of the live interaction capability) online instruction in addition to face-to-face instruction. In this case, students attending a seminar in a university venue or from a distance will also conduct study using online resources. As such, they may access instructional materials asynchronously, but can also engage in synchronous (real-time) communications with the instructor and other students using various types of email, chat or social media applications.

Dr Janet Macdonald, author of *Blended Learning and Online Tutoring*, points out that one of the primary challenges facing the seminar leader is to determine what parts of the seminar are amenable to synchronous (or asynchronous) access and which are better served by face-to-face meetings. More often than not, this decision is based on the limitations of the technology, rather than the content of the seminar. If, for example, the technology is unable to support certain visual and/or audio media applications required for the seminar, such sessions would probably be best served by having students attend the face-to-face meeting.[4] That said, Macdonald also notes that certain discussions, such as those associated with complex subject matter, are better served by face-to-face meetings.[5]

Ultimately, the seminar leader must determine what he or she believes to be the best blend of media and technologies for use in a seminar. How to do so in an effective manner is the trick, for 'no single model or blend of media fits all' programs.[6]

Research suggests that the increased use of blended learning (and, with it, blended seminars) in higher learning will foster a change in the traditional knowledge, skills and abilities associated with seminar leaders. In addition to those already described earlier in this book, seminar leaders will also have to possess the ability to be adept in creating and/or managing various types of evolving technologies. Further, seminar leaders may have to take on various additional instructional skills, including coaching, mentoring and counselling.[7]

▶ Summary

Students who otherwise are unable to attend your seminar in person have the ability to participate from afar via internet-based DL. The capabilities of DL software are such that you and your seminar students are now able to interact in real time with students taking the seminar from other locations. Distance learning software also offers you the ability to record your seminars for later and repeated viewing. There are, of course, advantages and disadvantages associated with every new educational technology; distance learning is no exception, as this chapter has emphasized.

This chapter also discussed the increasingly popular use of 'blended' learning – the combined use of various media and technologies together with synchronous and asynchronous DL capabilities to create an effective learning environment. As seminar leader, you must determine the proper mix and use of media and technologies to best serve your educational goals and the needs of your students.

KEY CHAPTER TAKEAWAYS

▶ The dramatic growth of DL is likely to continue for the foreseeable future. Seminar leaders who lack experience teaching in this way will find their professional opportunities diminish.

▶ As with any other technology-dependent mode of instruction, DL has its share of advantages and disadvantages. Its chief advantage is its ability to link geographically dispersed students in virtual classrooms; its main disadvantage is that the benefits of face-to-face communication are either lost, or otherwise attenuated.

▶ The modalities of DL increase the potential for cultural misunderstandings between the instructor and students, and among students themselves. The seminar instructor must therefore take proactive measures to reduce the likelihood of such problems.

▶ Blended seminars are becoming increasingly popular. They provide an opportunity to maximize the advantages of both DL and face-to-face seminar instruction.

9 End-of-course pitfalls

Whether your course lasts a few weeks or several months, one of the ongoing challenges facing you, as the instructor, is that of keeping your participants interested and actively involved throughout the entire duration of the seminar. Not an easy task – and one, that if not successfully addressed, can result in a seminar that, after some time, becomes stagnant, boring and no longer an effective means for learning. As we have already seen, passive students – those not actively engaged in seminar discussions – tend to become detached from the seminar proceedings; a problem that could lead to disinterest and complacency.

How, then, can you as seminar leader, help to keep your students' attention focused and their interest piqued until the very end of the course? We have already discussed a number of ways of achieving this in earlier chapters, where we noted the importance of developing effective facilitation skills. We saw that you must first create a strong foundation with which you, as facilitator, empower your students to play active and ongoing roles in the discourse. You were shown that on this foundation, it is necessary to build structural supports to maintain seminar integrity.

We observed that interpersonal dynamics between you, as leader, and your students, as participants, must remain flexible, adaptable and reinforcing. We also noted that, in the conduct of your seminar, it is your responsibility to create a learning environment that is open and creative; one that requires the active and ongoing participation of each and every participant. But this is not enough.

This chapter will address, in a detailed fashion, the various traps that may cause otherwise superior seminars to lose momentum toward the end of the course and to drain the creative forces that animate inquiry-based learning. These traps include instructor complacency – real or perceived; student anxiety about end-of-course assignments; and final seminars that, by abandoning the best practices so successfully used during the earlier meetings, lose momentum and lose student interest. Let us examine each of these problems in turn, as well as preventive and remedial measures with which to address them.

▶ The dangers of complacency

Let us imagine your seminar has just a few classes remaining. By now, you have seen how applying the many 'best practices' associated with effective inquiry-based learning outlined in this book has helped to make your seminar a productive and an enjoyable learning experience, both for yourself and your students. Except for the inevitable glitch here or there, it has all run smoothly, and you believe a successful finish is a given.

If this is your mindset, then be very careful, because your seminar is in danger of faltering even at this late stage. You have succumbed to possibly one of the greatest hazards that can befall a seminar leader – that of complacency, the state of contentedness and ease whereby one becomes less 'situationally aware' of one's actions (and their impacts on others) and, thus, less attentive to possible problems associated with one's behaviours.[1]

Consider the conductor of an orchestra or choir who fails to keep his ensemble under complete control until the silence after the last beat of the last movement. An otherwise perfectly played symphony can be ruined should the final chord be performed incorrectly. Think that is unduly harsh? It may well be, but the fact is you face a similar challenge as a seminar leader. You have built your entire seminar on those best practices specifically designed to keep your students actively involved in the dialogue. If your students perceive – rightly or wrongly – that you are becoming complacent towards the end of the course, the consequences will be devastating.

In this situation, some of your students may become complacent themselves, concluding that if you do not care about a strong finish, there is no reason why they should do so. Others may experience an opposite reaction and become anxious, especially if they believe you no longer care about their performance. But this is not all. To the extent that you have become complacent, it will be more difficult for you to discern your students' concerns, and thereby increase the potential for miscommunication.

There will be some variation among your students and how they approach the end of the course, quite apart from their perceptions of you. Your 'seminar superstars' – those who have been active contributors and excelled throughout – will have little difficulty making valuable contributions right up to the final moments of the last seminar meeting; others may mentally 'check out' early for all sorts of reasons; still others may be consumed with worries about the course grade and the final assignments, thereby distracting them from the materials being discussed.

How, then, to avoid the dangers of complacency for you and your students? Here are some tips.

Maintain your enthusiasm

Maintaining a high and ongoing level of enthusiasm throughout the seminar over the course of several months can be a real, and at times daunting, challenge.[2] This is understandable, given that you have devoted many hours to developing the course, leading the discussions, addressing students concerns both small and large, not to mention attending to all your other professional and personal responsibilities. Such a workload can take its toll, sapping your energy and enthusiasm as the semester winds to a close.

There are several things you can do to maintain your energy level. One key to maintaining your enthusiasm is to stay healthy, especially eating well and getting sufficient sleep. The mental and physical benefits of exercise are well-documented, so following a fitness programme is highly recommended.

You also need to be intellectually committed to making the closing seminars as dynamic and compelling as your opening ones. Track and field coaches always tell their sprinters to 'run through' the finish line, lest they consciously or unconsciously ease up prior to crossing it. This is also excellent advice for seminar instructors. Commit yourself to promoting a robust dialogue and interaction with your seminar students right up to the final bell.

Remain attentive to your students' needs

Maintaining student enthusiasm at this critical stage of the course is easier said than done. You must also keep in mind that, in addition to your seminar, your students may be engaged in numerous other courses and activities, both professional and personal. Adult students (especially those participating in the seminar by means of DL) may also have careers and families. Taking a seminar course or two in addition to these other ongoing responsibilities can prove taxing, both emotionally and physically. It is therefore critical that you acknowledge the reality of such competing demands and time commitments.

Showing empathy with respect to your students' busy schedules will strengthen the instructor–student bond you have already established. Make them aware that you understand that they have these many concurrent responsibilities, and that you appreciate their continued attention and participation. Reinforce the notion that they have given much time and effort to be a part of the seminar and that their input has contributed to its success. In this way, you can leverage the reality of such competing demands to help your students to focus on what is really important as the course draws to a close.

> **End-of-course pitfalls**
>
> You risk a poor finish if your seminar students:
>
> ▶ underestimate – or overestimate – what they have learned
>
> ▶ are confused about how the course is supposed to tie together
>
> ▶ tune out at the worst possible moment
>
> ▶ feel anxious about the final assignment.

Your students may be confused about how the course is supposed to tie together

To avoid this trap, you need to devote some time in the final sessions to pulling together different conceptual threads of the course. These are your last opportunities to emphasize key points and to help bring any unresolved discussions to closure. In guiding the seminar 'wrap-up', the emphasis should always be on your students – their comments, insights and contributions. You will want to retrace the intellectual path your students took, asking them to recall key themes and concepts.

Remember that some subjects lend themselves more readily to a tidy summary than others. Some sessions may even generate more questions than answers during the course of a semester, so you will need to manage expectations. An introductory course in philosophy – or even an advanced course for that matter – is not going to resolve, once and for all, the meaning of human existence.

Remember also that you are not the focal point of what is transpiring in the classroom. You are there to teach, to lead, to guide and to facilitate, not to lecture. As such, all of your attentions and activities must remain student-centred. You have maintained this focus since the beginning of the course, so do not abandon it now at the end. You should therefore avoid the temptation of handing your students a tidy summary of the course during the final seminar meeting. Instead, spend your time and effort drawing it out of them.

Students may underestimate – or overestimate – what they have learned

Some students may underestimate all the intellectual ground that they have covered during the course. Your closing sessions provide an excellent opportunity to remind them of their progress. As an instructor, you will have a better perspective of your students' progress than they will. You can take them back to the beginning of the semester, asking them to recall what they knew (and did not know) about the subject matter at that time. Your students may recall the substance of these early sessions as being fairly basic, but this is actually a positive sign because it serves to underscore how their subsequent understanding has grown deeper and more nuanced.

Conversely, some of your students may overestimate what they have learned. Intellectual hubris leads to all sorts of undesirable problems. In extreme cases, students may conclude they have learned everything there is to know of importance about a particular topic, or perhaps that the assigned readings represent the 'final say' on the subject. Unless you happened to have a true genius in your class (a rare but welcome experience), the students described here tend to suffer from a rather inflated view of their own intellectual abilities, a superficial view of the subject matter, or possibly some combination of the two. If this is the case, then you will want to note their progress during the course, but also stress that the subject matter has wider and deeper contours than you have been able to cover in the course. The sidebar illustrates the danger of overestimating one's understanding and capabilities.

> ## An example of student 'overestimation'
>
> An adult student we shall call Naz was attending a course in Austria on the German language. It was an intense six-week seminar where the students from around the globe were forbidden to make even the slightest utterance in a language other than German. By the end of the course, Naz believed that he had acquired an excellent grasp of the German language.
>
> Very proud of himself indeed, Naz and some fellow students stopped at a bar to celebrate the end of the course. When the waitress

inquired what this student wanted to drink, he loudly proclaimed that he wanted a beer, naming the specific brewing company with his request. This he did in a very loud and rather boastful tone, such that not only his fellow students, but practically everyone in the bar would hear his order in spoken in perfect High German.

The waitress's eyes suddenly widened and she put her hand to her mouth. Patrons at other tables started to laugh, some so hard that they started to cry. The newly-graduated students, and especially Naz, were thoroughly perplexed, not understanding what had gone wrong. Why was everyone crying tears of laughter? Well, it seems that in demonstrating his bravado, Naz had made quite an error; rather than saying that he wanted a beer brewed by a specific company, he had actually declared to all within hearing that he wanted a beer brewed by a part of the male human body that one does not generally discuss outside of a class on physiology or sex education. It turns out that the name of the brewery and that part of the male anatomy sound quite similar, with only one final letter at the end determining the very different meanings (an 'R' at the end of the name of the brewery, an 'L' at the end of the male appendage). Once this error was made clear to the poor Naz, he spoke no more, remaining silent for the rest of that entire day ... overestimating no longer.[3]

Uncertainty about the final assignment

Uncertainty and anxiety about the final assignment is another pitfall that often confounds students approaching the end of the semester. Ideally, you will have clearly explained final assignment requirements at the beginning of the course, both orally and in the syllabus, thus making it unnecessary to revisit them in any great detail. But, despite all this preparation and your best intentions, your students may still have excessive worries about these assignments. These anxieties may be prompted by external demands that have nothing to do with your particular course.

Your aim here, to the maximum extent possible, is to remove these uncertainties and assuage their anxieties. As you approach the final phase of the course, ask your students directly if they have any questions about the final assignment. Some students may raise their concerns during a seminar meeting; others may wish to visit you during office hours. Take your students' concerns seriously, regardless of how they approach you. Reiterate your expectations about the final assignment. Make sure your students have a copy of the grading rubric you will use to evaluate the final assignment, and walk them through it, if you sense this is necessary.

Yet another risk is that a few of your students may 'tune out', if you have a final writing assignment which appears disconnected from your seminar discussions. In extreme cases, such students may not see the need even to attend your final seminars. To avoid this scenario, your final assignments should be written so that your students will need to draw upon the insights and contributions of the closing seminars. This will help provide your students with the incentive to remain fully engaged and eager to learn throughout the course.

▶ Keys to a strong finish

- Maintain the state of energy and enthusiasm that you have displayed all along.
- Remain creative, active and alert to students' needs.
- Make the final seminar meeting the highlight of your course.

Strive to make the final seminar meeting the highlight of your course

It is during the final seminar meeting that all that has come before must be brought back and tied together into a coherent form, demonstrating that the many discussions, debates, special lectures and activities were all directed to your goals and the expectations of your students. There are several important ways to fulfil this.

Reaffirm expectations
To avoid a weak finish, you need to articulate your clear expectation that each of your students will contribute to the seminar discussions right up to the end of the final session. This is something that should have probably already been emphasized throughout the course, especially if you followed our earlier suggestions associated with the conduct of the first seminar meeting. As you approach the final seminars, now is the time to reaffirm your expectation that the students will finish strongly.

Tie together loose threads
Your job, as seminar leader, has been to guide your students in such a way that they see how even the varied, seemingly unrelated threads

of the course form part of a coherent tapestry. This can be a relatively straightforward task, if you have been discussing a single topic in depth. However, bringing all that has come before to a satisfying close may not be so simple, especially if your seminar topics have been quite varied.

Prepare diligently

Remember how much time and effort you put into planning the first seminar session? Strive to bring the same level of preparation to your final seminar, and you will find the pay-off well worth the effort. The final seminar is definitely not one that you want to improve or prepare for at the last minute. In fact, you should have a fairly clear idea of where you wish the course to conclude even before it begins, which brings us to the issue of course objectives.

Review course objectives

The summary session should review the course objectives and recurring themes throughout the course. Of course, you could provide all this for them given your academic expertise, but that would undermine the student-centred, active-learning model that you have sought to nurture throughout the course. To re-emphasize, you want to draw these points out of your students through questioning, not lecturing. And, if it turns out that the course did not quite hit the target with respect to all the course objectives, then you should freely admit this. Students will respect your candour.

Encourage feedback

As will be emphasized in Chapter 10, soliciting student feedback is an essential ingredient of a successful seminar. As you conduct the seminar wrap-up, make sure you solicit their views on how well the course achieved its objectives. There is a strong likelihood that, even if the class achieved all its objectives, it probably covered some of them better than others. If there was some element of a particular meeting or discussion that requires clarification, this would be a good time to do so.

Asking your students to provide oral feedback will reaffirm that you value their opinions. Moreover, this informal feedback can help prime them for whatever end-of-course critique you or your department have prepared for them. You will want to ensure the survey is undertaken anonymously to maintain the integrity of the process.

To encourage discussion, you may raise the following questions:

- Which of the classes did you find to be especially interesting?
- If you were the seminar leader, what aspects of the seminar would you change?
- What did you find to be the least and most valuable elements of the course?
- What surprised you about the course?

While some students may be loath to discuss these thoughts openly (especially those that may cast a negative light of some sort), others will have no compunction about telling you what aspects of the seminar they found most appealing and those they found to be less so. If you would like clarification of any criticism they raise, then make this known immediately and in a non-judgemental manner. Regardless of their responses, your countenance and demeanour should remain neutral and pleasant throughout, thanking them for their comments and showing appreciation for their candour.

This is another place where the around-the-room technique discussed in Chapter 5 can be very useful, especially if your seminar is relatively small and there is sufficient time to solicit feedback from all the participants.

Show your appreciation

Yet another technique to help ensure the seminar finishes on a strong note is to thank your students for all of the time and hard work that they put into making the seminar a success. Let them know how delighted you are that they participated in the discussions and debates. Praise them for their creativity and thoughtfulness. Equally important, you should candidly acknowledge any rough spots the seminar experienced during the semester – even the best seminars have a few. These rough spots can provide valuable learning experiences, provided you help the students put them into a larger perspective.

Praising your students in this manner is not meant to influence their opinions of you and/or the seminar. Rather, doing so will reinforce the notion that they were the focal point of the seminar. For those in the seminar group that contributed on a steady ongoing basis – those students on whom you could usually depend to generate discussion or debate, no matter what the topic (and there will be a few) – then such praise will be taken by them as a 'reward' for a job well done. For those whose contributions were there but limited, such reinforcement may provide the incentive to contribute at greater levels during seminars to come.

Whet their appetite

As you bring the final meeting to a close, you want to instil in your students the desire to return for additional study. Praise them for what they have accomplished during the seminar, but also tell them that their inquiry should not just stop when they leave the seminar room for the last time. There remain many areas to be discussed and questions to answer, and you should take a moment to point out the avenues for further research and discourse. If a seminar is being planned, by either you or a colleague, that builds on the one that you have just led, then by all means let your students know of this.

Encourage students to stay in contact

Let your students know that they are welcome to stay in contact with you after the completion of the seminar. In this way, you show your students that you remain interested in their academic and professional welfare, even when they are no longer under your wing.

Of course, human nature being what it is, not all of your students will want to stay in touch with you, but some will. They will want to share with you their academic or professional successes and failures. They may seek out your advice on a matter related to what was covered during your seminar. Still others may ask you to provide mentorship, or perhaps a written reference. All of these types of continued contacts can prove very rewarding, as they suggest that, in some way, you have left some enduring positive impacts on your students. There is nothing more that an educator can wish.

Your seminar, then, should close in such a manner that your students will leave it feeling that they have had an invaluable learning experience that can last long after the end of the seminar, that they wish to learn more about what has been discussed, and that others would benefit by taking this seminar with you, should it once again be offered. Such are some of the indicators that your seminar has been a success. However, as we will see in Chapter 10, there are a number of other ways to determine whether you have, indeed, led a successful seminar.

Encourage your students to reflect on the broader significance of the course

As the final seminar draws to a close, you should strive to say a few words about the broader significance of the course. You can encourage your students to revisit key texts in the future, noting that they are likely to gain even more insight – both about themselves and the subject matter – with the passage of time. In this way, the key texts provide the students with a mirror to assess their own intellectual growth and development. This is an excellent opportunity to remind your students about the importance and rewards of being a lifelong learner.

You may wish to ask your students to reflect how the course has affected them personally. For some, it may influence their future course of study at the university. For others, the course may even influence their career choice. You may not receive immediate feedback from such far-reaching questions – in some cases it will take some time for your students to think through the broader significance of what they have achieved – but these questions are still worth raising. The best instructors are adept in seeding questions in the same way a farmer plants his crop, with great care and diligence. You should seek to do the same.

▶ Summary

The successful seminar leader knows that the positive learning cycle must be maintained and reinforced during each and every seminar meeting, from the first to last. Yet, it is during the final meetings of the seminar that, for a host of reasons, the ability to maintain the positive learning cycle and seminar bond with students can become tenuous and vulnerable to collapse. As this chapter makes clear, this need not happen. In applying the strategies described above, you can ensure that your students recognize that all they had accomplished during the seminar had finally reached a salient logical endpoint; one where many questions were resolved and others were not. Both you and your students should be satisfied and edified, having reached your goals, or (if not) achieving as many of your academic objectives as possible.

Your subjective assessment of the seminar and student participation may be all that you need to affirm the success of the course. Yet, there are other, more empirical approaches that can, and should, be taken to ensure that success has been achieved; you do not want to wait until the end of the final session to discover that one or more of your students had become lost, disengaged, or failed to understand what was transpiring. It is, from the first session, absolutely critical that you provide the means to determine the state of comprehension and learning, and for you to assess student performance. In Chapter

10, we will discuss some of the ways to measure these outcomes in order to know truly whether or not your seminar has been a success.

KEY CHAPTER TAKEAWAYS

▶ A strong finish can reinforce earlier seminar success; a weak finish will leave your students disappointed and confused.

▶ Be sure to provide your students with a sense of perspective as the course draws to a close, reminding students what they have learned and achieved during the semester.

▶ Leave the door open to future contact, since this reinforces the message that you care about your students, and it may provide you with invaluable feedback later on.

▶ As best you can, assuage student concerns about the final assignment(s) so that this does not detract from the final seminar discussions.

10 Measure outcomes

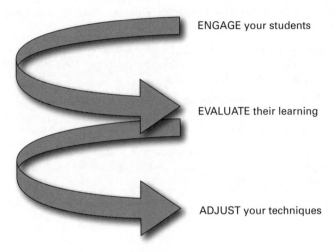

ENGAGE your students

EVALUATE their learning

ADJUST your techniques

Figure 10.1 Measuring outcomes

Let us imagine that you have managed to involve virtually all your students in your early seminar meetings. That is definitely a plus, but it only tells a partial story. The number of students engaging in seminar dialogue is but one of several metrics you should consider in evaluating your seminar.

By 'metric' we mean a measurement of learning effectiveness. Some metrics can be quantified with precision; others are more subjective and require a greater degree of interpretation. A test that involves factual questions is an example of the former; an essay, the latter.

You should use metrics for yourself and for your students – from the very first day of class; throughout the course; and, whenever possible, even after its conclusion. As individual yardsticks, metrics combine to provide assessments which provide a larger and broader perspective on learning effectiveness. These assessments, in turn, can have a powerful impact on learning behaviour within the framework of inquiry-based learning.[1]

Assessments fall into two broad categories, depending on their timing and purpose. Formative assessments are diagnostic in nature; they are used early in seminars to evaluate the students' skills, knowledge and abilities prior to learning the material. Summative assessments are used towards the end of instruction – whether for a particular class, block of instruction, or the course itself – to measure what has been learned.

Formative and summative assessments must be used in tandem to measure progress over a period of time. The goal here is to measure how well your students are learning individually and collaboratively[2] – much easier said than done. The key is to make your course objectives measurable, for otherwise your efforts to evaluate the effectiveness of your course will be speculative, at best.

As emphasized in the Chapter 2 on seminar preparations, the course objectives provide navigational beacons for you and your students. Every seminar discussion should link to the course objectives. For this reason, you want to take great care in formulating your course objectives. If you include vague phrasings, then measuring success – or the lack thereof – becomes problematic.

Example 1

Class objective: Understand the causes of the French Revolution.

The phrasing here is vague. A student's 'understanding' may be deep and penetrating; it may be shallow and superficial. The use of the word 'understanding' here does little to differentiate between these two extremes. Now consider an alternative construction.

Example 2

Class objective: Summarize competing theories on the causes of the French Revolution.

This formulation is more precise. In asking students to summarize 'competing theories', you will get a much clearer sense of their depth of understanding the topic.

▶ Meaning of success

One of the greatest challenges with respect to measuring seminar success is that the term 'success' often means different things to administrators, instructors and students. Administrators normally consider enrolment, attendance and graduation rates to be measures of success. Some of your students may consider success to mean simply attaining a passing grade in the course. Others may take a more ambitious view of what constitutes success, and consider how the course will help them prepare for a specific career. For this reason, it is useful to make clear to your students what you consider to be a successful seminar. This should be communicated both in the syllabus and orally at the beginning of the course. This vision, in turn, will help you explain the evaluation process to your students.

▶ Grading rubrics

As for evaluating specific assignments, you should develop rubrics that specify how each of them will be graded.[3] Rubrics are simply tools that help to formulate assessments. Let us consider how instructors should evaluate seminar participation. Instructors should note the frequency of participation, realizing this is but one metric for evaluating your seminar students. You will also want to focus on the quality and the quantity of the seminar contributions, as outlined in Table 10.1. For example, a student who has not undertaken the reading and offers

Table 10.1 Rubric for evaluating class contributions

Graded element	Components	Percentage of grade
Frequency of participation	How often does the student engage in dialogue?	25
Value of participation	Are the contributions thoughtful? Do they reflect an appreciation for the readings? Do they address the learning objectives for the class?	25
Courtesy towards others	Does the student interrupt others? Does the student respect the opinions of others, even if he or she disagrees with them?	25
Listening skills	Does the student reflect on the comments of others?	25

nothing more than uninformed opinions should not be rewarded, however forcefully they are presented. Neither should a student who rarely speaks receive a high seminar participation grade, even if his or her occasional comments are well-informed and well-reasoned. Such students can prove to be quite frustrating to their instructors, since they obviously have the potential to contribute much more to the seminar but, for whatever reason, are unable or elect not to do so.

Rubrics help to evaluate distinctive elements of seminar participation, as well as their relative importance to one another.

▶ Examinations and papers

Graded course requirements (such as exams, quizzes and papers) can also help gauge the nature and scope of learning. However, the use of end-of-course graded assignments as the sole form of assessment should be avoided, as this approach may direct student attention principally towards doing well on such assignments, rather than participating in open dialogue throughout the course. Moreover, relying solely on end-of-course assignments does not leave any time for you to refocus the seminar in the event that the grades from such assignments suggest that your students may not have actually learned the material.

The results of a short paper or written exam early in the course can provide you with a much earlier assessment of how well the course is meeting its objectives, thus allowing for course corrections, as needed.

The paper assignments should be linked with the discussions in class. This will reinforce the importance of student contributions to the seminar discussions in a real and tangible manner. You can highlight linkages for your students by reminding them of specific discussion points.

Paper Assignment Example 1

In seminar, we have discussed the importance of the id, ego and superego in modern psychology. Now apply these concepts to a contemporary leader ...

Paper Assignment Example 2

In our seminar discussions, some students emphasized the social costs of new economic programmes, while other students stressed the economic costs of new social programmes. Imagine that now you are mayor of a large city. Which approach would you take? Explain.

You should always provide some feedback in seminar on the results of such graded assignments. This type of openness is helpful to students who may be wondering about their performance relative to the rest of the group. There is, of course, always the possibility that such a discussion may evoke feelings of envy or inferiority among the more insecure students, but you can manage this by choosing your words carefully to encourage not only the students who did well, but also those who did not. This openness also provides you with an opportunity to ask questions that will help you understand their performance even better.

Example 1

We discussed the underlying causes of Imperial Rome's prosperity at length in seminar, so I am a little surprised that only a few papers referenced this historical analysis. Perhaps the assignment could have been worded better? What do you think?

Example 2

Our seminar discussion last week addressed the role of monarchy in the twenty-first century. Our discussions suggested some sharp divisions in public opinion that only a few students deemed important in their papers. Why?

Short assignments early in the course provide you with the opportunity to give your students valuable feedback, thereby drawing their attention to trends – both good and bad – that can assist them as they prepare for their next assignment. Establishing such a feedback loop is, thus, an important part of the seminar-based learning cycle.

► Informal indicators of success

There will always be an element of subjectivity in measuring academic performance. Informal indicators fall into this category. Even though they cannot be quantified with any precision, informal indicators can still provide insight into your course. Consider the following indicators:

- *Do some students show up early for class?* This can be a very good sign, especially if the students appear eager to engage in conversation. Conversely, if students arrive at the last minute, or late, this may signal disinterest or apathy.
- *Do the students engage one another – and with the instructor – on issues of substance during breaks?* It is a very positive sign if the seminar discussion 'spills over' into break time, since this reflects a high level of interest and engagement.
- *Do some students linger after your seminar class to engage in follow-on discussions with you or their fellow students?* However, do not assume the worst, if some of your students appear to rush out of the door. It may simply be that they have another class shortly afterwards across campus and lingering is not an option.
- *Do your seminar students approach you during office hours to discuss the course?* If no one calls in during office hours, then perhaps your students consider you intimidating or overbearing.

If the answer to most of these questions is 'yes', then this is a very good sign. If most of the answers are negative, however, then you should want to take a look in the mirror to consider how best to stimulate greater interest and engagement in your course.

▶ Taking the pulse – early and often

Your feedback provides an important means by which to measure the success of your seminar. If your assessment of the situation is generally accurate, then the feedback is more likely to be received as intended. Students will recognize your good intentions and ability to remedy whatever may be askew in the seminar. On the other hand, if your feedback appears to generate angst or confusion, then it is likely that you are missing the overall target.

You should be open to providing and receiving feedback throughout the course. This is especially true after each of your first few sessions. If this seminar is off to a poor start, for whatever reason, then it is best to address the problems as soon as possible, since problems that are allowed to fester tend to grow worse over time. On the other hand, if your seminar is off to a strong start, then seize this opportunity to reinforce the positive learning cycle by emphasizing the positives and challenging your students to elevate their performance to an even higher level.

Remember, regardless of how well you may think your seminar is progressing, there is always room for improvement. For this reason, you should avoid thinking to yourself – let alone saying to your students – that the seminar is going well. This can lead to complacency – both for you and your students – which usually signals trouble.

▶ Providing feedback to groups and to individuals

Seminar problems generally fall into two categories. First, they may be of a general nature, affecting all or most of your students. Others may be specific to a single student, or to perhaps a small number of students. Whatever the nature of the problem(s) and however many students are involved, you must address these problems with equal seriousness and provide feedback.

Example 1

We have had some constructive seminar discussions thus far, but our analysis could be much deeper. For instance, in discussing the French Revolution last week, no one really considered the economic dimension that was stressed in your readings. Remember, the readings provide fuel for our discussions, so I expect you to take them seriously.

Consider, though, that by emphasizing the 'we' pronoun, you reinforce the collaborative nature of the learning.

Example 2

We are being too easy on the authors we are reading. You are doing an excellent job summarizing their views, but we need to think more deeply about the underlying assumptions and premises that underlie these arguments.

If the problem affects a handful of students, you should couch any such admonitions so that students will understand the intent of your message as being directed towards them without having to single them out by name.

Example 3

Some of you turned in your homework assignment last week very late.
For those that did so, remember that this will have an impact on your
overall course grade, as noted in our syllabus. And for those of you
have who turned the assignment in on time, keep up the great work!

Unless a student commits a gross infraction in seminar that merits immediate correction, you should never single out a student for correction when critiquing the group as a whole.[4] This will embarrass the student in front of his or her peer group, which is certain to alienate the student. It will also have a chilling effect on students who may otherwise want to engage in the seminar dialogue.

If there is an obvious problem concerning just one student, it is better to counsel the student outside the seminar room. For example, if John has a bad habit of falling asleep in seminar and you mention the importance of staying awake, you can be sure that everyone in the seminar room, including John, will quickly discern that you are talking about him.

Culturally diverse students

There are limits to measuring learning outcomes. For instance, metrics that work well for one demographic of students may not work as well for another. If your seminar group includes a number of international students, you will need to take this into account in developing your assessment metrics. This does not mean lowering standards. You will, however, need to think about how cultural differences may impede an international student from reaching his or her potential in your seminar. For example, imagine that some of your international students are unfamiliar with inquiry-based learning and the give-and-take dialogue that characterizes the Socratic seminar. You may need to provide some individual counselling with these students, to explain the nature of open non-attribution discourse, and to assure them that their inputs would never result in any form of punitive action. Even with such information, some students may remain uncomfortable in this new academic environment. You may therefore have to spend some extra time during the first couple of seminar sessions to explain the nature of seminar discussion and your expectations for participation.

You should emphasize that you are not disparaging anyone's culture. On the contrary, you must make it clear to your international students that you welcome the new perspectives into the classroom, since they will enrich everyone's learning experience. Having done this, you must also articulate the standards for your seminar class, while noting that they may well differ from the norms and expectations to which some students are accustomed.

Cultural differences and feedback

You should realize that students from different cultures will not be equally comfortable in providing feedback. Some may be loath to say anything critical about the course, since this is not part of their cultural tradition.

In some cultures, the purpose of education is simply one of transmission of knowledge from the instructor to the student. The instructor is treated with great deference and respect, and is not someone to be questioned or challenged. In such settings, the idea of collaborative learning, as defined in this text, can be alien – even quite frightening – to students, regardless of their natural abilities. Students from formerly communist countries, for instance, often fall into this category. Unfortunately, this transmit–receive model of education remains entrenched in the educational cultures of their home countries.

Cultural awareness, therefore, is a must for professors who are responsible for teaching a diverse range of students. But this awareness does not mean lowering standards or sacrificing your course objectives. You should explain the Western tradition of using the Socratic Dialogue at the outset of the course, and then model it by questioning your students in a respectful yet challenging manner.

Coping with lack of feedback

Imagine that you encounter a 'deafening' silence when you ask your students how they think the seminar is progressing. This is a serious problem, since silence could mean a host of things – few of which are likely to be positive. It may mean your students are so thrilled that they are left speechless (unlikely)! Or, perhaps it means that they are bored, dissatisfied and feel they are wasting their time with each moment they stay in your seminar room (just as unlikely). It is probable that the majority of the students fail to respond because they do not know how to formulate their responses tactfully, do not wish to do so in a public forum where they can be identified as having made (usually, less than positive) comments, or are just uncomfortable participating at all. You are therefore left with just a few (typically positive) comments that are made and must 'guess' as to the responses from your uncooperative students.

Such guessing is dangerous because it usually leads to self-generated subjective appraisals that lack foundations in rationale and could prove destructive to the positive learning cycle. To avoid the pitfalls associated with such guesswork, you should always seek out various means of obtaining constructive feedback from your participants.

As the seminar leader, you are ultimately responsible for creating conditions in which students feel comfortable providing you with feedback. In the absence of such conditions, it will be far more difficult to measure success or failure. At the outset of the course, you should always stress to the participants that they are encouraged to approach you at any time during the semester, if they are experiencing difficulties. You should provide them with your contact information at the first meeting – office phone and email – so they know how and when to reach you, as needed.

Always pay close attention to the issues your students raise with you. If one student conveys dissatisfaction with the course, for whatever reason, it is always possible that other students feel the same way, but have yet to articulate this.

As your course unfolds, you should consider questioning some of your more accomplished seminar students 'offline' to see how they think the seminar is progressing. Your questions should be open-ended and provide an invitation for students to comment on any aspect of the seminar. There are a variety of ways you can do this. You could casually approach them in the hallway, or perhaps right after class. You could also ask the 'early birds' in your class what they think about the course, since they tend to be among the more serious students. The key point here is to be as informal as possible, since this will increase the likelihood that you will receive honest feedback.

You want to hear expressions like:

- 'To be honest, your seminar …'
- 'I really think this course …'
- 'Maybe I am the only one thinking this, but …'
- 'Please do not take offence, but this course …'

These comments are usually much more revealing than bland comments such as 'everything is good' or 'I am happy with the course'.

▶ Looking in the mirror

You are part of the equation when it comes to evaluating educational outcomes. You may be totally convinced that you are fostering good seminar discussions – and let's hope that, in most cases, you are indeed correct in your assessment! But even the best faculty members may have one (or more) blind spots regarding their abilities – or lack thereof.

Remember, there is no such thing as the perfect seminar instructor. Take a step back and consider how others may see you. Maybe you slip into lecture mode at the expense of the students? Perhaps your summaries at the end of seminar are a little too long? Or maybe you rely too heavily on just a handful of participants, instead of spreading the discussion around more evenly?

Taking an introspective look at yourself is one of the most difficult – yet, also, most important – things you can do as a seminar leader. To this end, you should consider indicators that things may be awry in your seminar.

Questions you should ask yourself on a regular basis:

- ▶ Do my students generally show up on time?

- ▶ Are some of my students frequently absent from seminar?

- ▶ Do all my students engage in the seminar discussion, or just a select handful?

- ▶ Do my questions normally foster a lively exchange of ideas, or seem to engender deadly silences?

- ▶ Do students readily approach me before and after class?

- ▶ Do my students ask questions after class, or race to leave?

- ▶ Who is doing most of the talking in seminar? Me or my students?

- ▶ Do my seminars engage all the students more or less equally in terms of their participation?

- ▶ Do I have an unusual number of students requesting office hours? (This can be a good or bad indicator, depending on why they are visiting your office.)

▶ Final seminar and survey

Your final seminar provides yet another avenue to solicit feedback. Oral comments by the students at the end of the course may be 'impressionistic' in nature, but they can also capture subtleties and otherwise hard-to-describe emotion-based intangibles that are more difficult to convey in standard surveys, or to recall at a later date.

The use of anonymous surveys can help to put your students at ease when they provide more formal feedback. You should require your students to submit their final survey after they take or submit their final graded assignment, since this will reduce any fear that anonymous comments may somehow be traced back to them.

If your department does not provide surveys for you to use, then you should consider drafting your own unless, for some reason, your university or college policies prohibit this. There are numerous online sites that assist with constructing academic surveys. Ideally, you could use an online platform for capturing student inputs anonymously, since this will improve your chances of receiving candid feedback.

▶ Summary technique

Another useful technique for evaluating learning is to call upon students to provide summaries at the end of individual seminars. As noted in Chapter 5, this technique can help your students develop the valuable skill of distilling key ideas into a short summary. This technique also provides you with a valuable tool to assess how well your students are learning.

You should model this technique for the first several sessions, and then make it clear that in the future, towards the end of the seminar, you will be asking one student to provide a short summary of what the class has discussed and learned.

You should first call on your more able and communicative students. This will help set a high standard for the others to follow, and for some to surpass. After the seminar is completed, you should encourage other students to ask questions, or to provide additional summary points, as needed. Then you should provide the closing, commending the student who provided the summary and, if necessary, adding some final points of your own. Your final words are especially important, if the student omits any key points and/or makes some sort of factual error that merits correction.

The summary technique is an excellent means to encourage your students to take ownership of the discussion. Students will quickly realize that only the best insights make it into the seminar summaries. You will also gain greater insight into how well the students are learning – both from the student summarizing the discussion, and from any subsequent comments from the other students.

▶ Reflective writing

Reflective writing assignments provide another avenue to evaluate your students. These assignments encourage students to consider how well the seminar is progressing, and to provide some introspection regarding their own performance. You should encourage your students to write in the first person singular 'I' to personalize their reflections as much as possible. You should also consider assigning this reflective assignment early in the semester to obtain an impression of how well your seminar techniques are working. This has the added benefit of forcing the students to reflect on the nature of learning.[5]

Example 1

Reflect on our seminar discussions thus far. What are you learning about yourself and your peers?

Example 2

Reflect on your expectations coming into the course. Has the course met your expectations thus far? Are you meeting your own expectations in terms of seminar contributions? Explain.

Example 3

Reflect on the dynamics within our seminar room. Do you feel comfortable sharing your views in this forum? Has your comfort level changed during the course?

These types of questions are not a standard 'evaluate this' or 'analyze that' assignment that focuses on the substance of the course. Clearly, they are more personal in nature, asking students to be honest and frank in the evaluation of their own performance in relation to the learning process itself.

This type of higher order reflection will be new and challenging to some of your students. As always, you will need to filter the results with a discerning eye. Do not be surprised if some of the comments are critical of your instruction. This is to be expected, especially from students who may not be acquainted, or comfortable, with the Socratic Method, and it suggests that they are taking the assignments seriously. (It is better to receive criticism than apathetic replies, since the latter make learning downright tedious, if not impossible.)

There are some variations on the reflective writing assignment you can use to assess how well your students are learning. For example, you could ask the students to maintain a blog or journal throughout the entire course. If you opt for something like this, then you must clearly specify how often you will read and evaluate student entries.

The reflective writing exercises will provide you with greater insight into how your students are adapting to the seminar. Reflections that are rich with insights and self-discovery provide a good indicator that your students are constructively engaged in the learning process. In many cases, the results of the reflective writing assignment will match what you see in the seminar room. Students who are making valuable contributions in class are likely to be the same students who are reflecting at a deep level. In other cases, you may find that some of your less vocal students are, nonetheless, reflecting at an equally deep level. Your ability to provide them complementary feedback on their blog or journal entries provides an opening for you to draw them out more during the seminar discussions.

▶ Feedback loops and measuring outcomes

Your aim should be to seek as much feedback as possible from your students. This does not, however, mean that you have to react or respond to every piece of information. After all, some of the feedback may say more about the particular student than anything of substance about your seminar. Some complaints may be frivolous in nature, in which case you should remind the student on the importance of engaging in, and constructively contributing to, seminar discussions. Other seemingly frivolous complaints may mask a deeper problem. For instance, a student may complain about his seat being situated near the door when, in reality, his real grievance involves one of his neighbours. All such communications should be taken seriously. As such, you are challenged, as seminar leader, to understand the locus of these complaints and the nature of your intervention, if any.

Sometimes, when you least expect it, student feedback will come months or even years later, perhaps in the form of an appreciative email, letter or phone call. This type of feedback can be especially valuable, since it comes from the vantage point of a longer time horizon. If you are fortunate enough to receive delayed feedback, you should seize this opportunity to ask the former student some follow-on questions, both about the substance of what was learned and the learning techniques:

- Looking back, is there anything that the course missed?
- Are there any areas of the course you wished we had focused on more on? Focused on less?
- What seminar techniques to stimulate discussion did you find most helpful? Least helpful?

Some universities use formal surveys to seek periodic feedback from alumni. This can provide yet another window into the effectiveness of your seminar teaching, if the survey includes specific questions about specific courses. If you have the opportunity to help shape the questions to make them germane to your particular course, then by all means do so. After all, you will have the best insight into your course and its objectives.

▶ Asking for a second opinion

You may find it helpful to seek out the opinions of a more seasoned instructor, asking him or her to 'sit in' on a seminar as an observer. The individual should be someone whose judgement you trust. Ideally, this evaluation should take place early during the course, so there is ample time to make appropriate course corrections after receiving feedback. You should always note the presence of the individual at the outset of the seminar meeting, so that your students are not left guessing who the visitor is, or why they are there.

Example

Today, Professor Jones from our Political Science Department will be observing our seminar at my request. Sometimes instructors invite observers to provide feedback on the seminar. But don't worry … he will be assessing me, not you!

Afterwards, offer to buy your guest observer a cup of coffee and listen closely to what he or she has to say about your seminar leading techniques. Jot down the most important points, reflect on what the observer has suggested, and then consider modifying your techniques, if merited. Depending on the feedback, you may want to invite the same observer back later in the course to observe another seminar. This approach will provide the observer an opportunity to assess any adjustments you have made in your teaching techniques.

▶ The value of evaluations

You may view the time spent evaluating your students in seminar to be excessive. There is certainly an opportunity cost involved: the time you spend evaluating performance metrics is time not spent on instruction. But the potential gains are significant. By applying a variety of metrics, you will gain a more exact and comprehensive assessment of what your seminar students are learning. Most of your students will welcome this attention, because your efforts in this regard communicate that you care about them and their educational welfare. This, in turn, will assist your teaching efforts in the classroom – and thus provide your seminar with yet another positive learning cycle!

▶ How to avoid survey fatigue

While it is important to assess your students on a regular basis, you must take care not to overburden them with surveys, since this will diminish the value of the feedback. The result is often referred to as 'survey fatigue'. There are a number of things you can do to reduce the likelihood of survey fatigue, including communicating results and providing real-time feedback to your students on the surveys.[6]

► Summary

The time and effort required to measure outcomes can be frustrating at times, but this practice also yields important educational benefits. Simply put, this is the only way to take the guesswork out of educational effectiveness. There is, after all, a natural human tendency to rationalize one's own behaviour, and educators are no exception to this rule. Surveys provide an important check to such rosy self-assessments. They permit you to make tactical corrections to your course in a timely manner, if needed. More broadly, they provide the data to consider more long-term, strategic educational reforms.

Transparency is a virtue when it comes to soliciting and evaluating feedback. As noted earlier, explaining the rationale behind the surveys is an important means to mitigate the potential for survey fatigue. Equally important, your efforts to capture feedback will send a deeper message that you really do care about the students and their perceptions of the course. Your students, in turn, will respond positively to your sincere and sustained attention.

KEY CHAPTER TAKEAWAYS

▶ Without metrics to evaluate your course, you will lack a clear sense of whether your seminar is hitting its intended target.

▶ You should provide your students rubrics for all graded elements of the course.

▶ Seek out formal and informal feedback early in the course. Partial feedback early in the course is more valuable than extensive feedback later in the course, when it becomes too late to make changes.

▶ Post-course feedback can be especially valuable, since it typically provides a broader perspective.

▶ Not every student criticism requires a course correction. Student feedback should always be filtered to separate routine grumbling from more serious concerns.

▶ In assessing your own effectiveness, remember that humility and self-awareness are virtues, not weaknesses.

▶ Seasoned colleagues can provide a valuable quality-control check on your seminar, so do not hesitate to invite them to observe your seminar.

11 Some final thoughts and suggestions

If leading seminars were easy, this book would be neither necessary nor interesting. The fact is, effective seminar leading involves a good deal of sweat equity. Hard work and preparation are essential, especially for instructors who have not had the benefit of learning from positive role models during their formative educational experiences. But it is also richly rewarding for instructors who are willing to learn best practices and apply them in the seminar room.

It is hard to overstate the potential impact your seminar can have on students. A well-planned and executed seminar will bolster their critical learning skills and confidence, enabling them to approach complex issues, both individually and collaboratively, whatever your subject matter. They will come to appreciate inquiry-based learning, which is a framework they will carry with them well beyond the course.

This text has sought to capture many of the best practices for seminar learning, and to illustrate them with real-world examples. As emphasized throughout this handbook, there is no such thing as a 'cookie-cutter' approach when it comes to leading seminars. Now it is up to you to apply these techniques in your seminar, a challenge which is admittedly easier to articulate than to accomplish. The application of best practices always requires judgement and discernment because the specific context of your seminar will vary depending on the composition of your seminar. Let the spirit of inquiry-based learning guide you in developing your seminar leading skills.

Here are some specific suggestions to help you do this.

First, make a list of the best practices from this book, your mentors and other sources that you wish to apply to your next seminar course. The very act of making this list will help you to reflect on how to apply them in your seminar room.

Second, prior to the start of your next seminar, list three to five specific areas where you want to improve your seminar teaching. These areas can be based on your own (albeit subjective) self-evaluation, feedback from fellow colleagues, formal performance appraisals, or student feedback (or some combination of all four). Now jot down some ideas on how to make these improvements, and develop a plan for implementation (see Table 11.1). Create some goals that you wish to achieve. The key here is to be realistic, for setting goals either too low or too high will set you up for failure. After the course concludes, revisit these goals, noting whether you achieved some or all of the goals. Note also how well you thought the ideas you implemented actually worked. Be honest with these post-seminar self-reviews, for they are critical in laying the foundations for future improvements.

Table 11.1 Example of a self-improvement plan

Areas for improvement	Strategy for improvement	Notes
Opening and closing my seminars in order to make them more focused.	I will rehearse my openings and closing remarks before seminar.	Use note cards, if necessary. Practice in front of the mirror and/or trusted colleague
Getting to know my students better in order to make them feel welcomed and at ease.	I will seek to engage my students in discussion immediately before and after class.	Ask about their hobbies, extra-curricular activities.
Formulating clear and measurable course objectives in order to provide my course with greater clarity and coherence.	Have a trusted peer review my draft objectives for clarity. Reassess how my course objectives support departmental and university objectives.	Review faculty handbook for guidance. Schedule chat with department head.

Third, remember that reflection is an essential component of learning. So, put this handbook down for a few days after you finish reading it; then, return to the text and review pages you have underlined, highlighted or tabbed for future reference. This approach will give your mind an opportunity to 'digest' what you have read. Taking a fresh look at passages or chapters you did not quite grasp on first reading may well appear clearer on reflection.

Fourth, recall the benefits of collaborative learning. So, discuss what you have learned from this book with one or more trusted colleagues who have also read it. They may have some additional insights for you to consider, based on their experience and reading of the text. Discussing the text with someone else will serve to deepen your understanding of it – and theirs as well.

It is important to remember that your efforts to become a better seminar leader will take some time, requiring both persistence and patience. The inquiry-based learning approach you seek to inculcate in your students should also inform your efforts to become a better teacher. You need to try different techniques to see what works best for your particular personality, teaching style and the curricular objectives are you seeking to achieve.

Do not be discouraged to find your journey is uneven at times, since trying new techniques carries both risks and rewards. Not every class is going to leave you and your students walking on air with exhilaration. You may, in fact, feel deflated at times. This is normal and part of the learning process, so do not expect perfection in the seminar room – from either yourself or your students; this only serves to set you up for certain disappointment.

You will make errors during your seminar. Everyone does. Yours may reflect poor decisions, a lack of, or inappropriate, application of your knowledge and/or skills, or even a failure to perceive the state of student–leader dynamics at a given time. You will either become aware of such errors yourself, or a student may bring them to your attention. In either case, you should quickly admit the misdemeanour and move forward. Though it sounds counterintuitive, your ability to exclaim 'Mea maxima culpa!' in public will actually enhance your credibility as an educator, since your students are smart enough to realize that perfect instructors do not exist in the real world. However, you can certainly approach this goal, for a small dose of humility can go a long way in creating – even enhancing – your credibility in the classroom. A little laughter directed at your expense can help establish your humanity, as well.

Example

Yesterday I tried to explain a point about economic theory by drawing an analogy between selling apples and manufacturing automobiles. Judging from your questions and quizzical expressions, it is evident that I succeeded only in confusing you. Allow me to give this analogy another go ...

or

Human beings are prone to making mistakes, as I proved yesterday in confusing the names of two minor eighteenth-century English poets! To make amends, I have written their names on the board along with some of their best-known works. I apologize for the confusion.

▶ Closing thoughts

Viewed from a broader perspective, the type of collaborative learning you can help promote in the seminar room is a powerful engine of human progress and growth. While individual genius certainly plays a role, collaborative efforts have also played a larger role in furthering the admittedly slow and uneven advance of civilization. You, too, can be a part of this grand tradition in your capacity as a seminar leader.

Naturally, no one can master all the techniques at once. Our own learning experiences as educators have been pockmarked with disappointments and setbacks. Best practices require practice over time. Therefore, keep this handbook close to you, both literally and figuratively. Mark it up and reflect on it. Revisit and reread it as necessary. Let it become both a navigational beacon to guide your professional growth and a mirror to evaluate your progress as a seminar leader. If, over time, techniques described in this book become second nature to you, then this means you have made considerable progress in developing your repertoire.

Remember that your work in the seminar room provides you with the privileged opportunity to touch the future by having a positive impact on your students. While there are striking examples of highly successful people who dropped out of college – Bill Gates of Microsoft fame comes to mind – these cases are well-known precisely because they are exceptionally rare. For every Gates, there are millions of other students who have diminished their career opportunities by dropping out. Finishing their education and doing well academically do not guarantee your students future job success, but they certainly improve the odds.

As an educator, you can play a tremendous role in improving these odds for your students. Students are much more likely to drop out when they do not feel connected to what they are studying. Students are also much more likely to feel connected in the seminar room than they would in the lecture hall, or engaged in independent study. This is yet another advantage of inquiry-based learning, as emphasized throughout the text. Direct and interactive dialogue involving instructors and students is what sets apart the seminar room from other educational approaches, such as lectures halls, self-study and peer-to-peer learning. In this way, you can instil in them a love of learning that will last a lifetime. In so doing, you will achieve something lasting and meaningful, which is no small achievement in a world where the fleeting and transient tend to dominate.

Now that you have read this text, you are primed to commence an exciting journey during which you will lead, guide, mentor, facilitate and enlighten. You will apply specific techniques, as well as the principles of inquiry-based learning, to a real setting. It is your passion for teaching, informed by best practices, that will take you from here. Share it with your students – for, in doing so, you will be creating for them an educational experience that they will long remember and cherish.

It's time to set sail. Let the adventure begin!

KEY CHAPTER TAKEAWAYS

▶ Remember that a little humility can go a long way in the classroom. If your standard for leading seminars is one of perfection, then you will surely be disappointed.

▶ Seek out opportunities to improve your teaching techniques at every turn.

▶ Examine the techniques of leaders who excel at teaching and inspiring, and adopt them for your own use in the seminar room.

▶ Remember that, as seminar leader, you are in a unique and privileged position to touch the future by instilling in your students a lifelong love of learning, as well as preparing them for life beyond the university.

Notes

▶ Introduction

1   We use the terms 'seminar leader', 'educator', 'instructor' and 'faculty' interchangeably throughout the text. Likewise, our book uses the terms 'student' and 'participant' as synonyms.

2   Some lecturers may permit a question-and-answer period following their presentation. But, even in these cases, the extent of student–faculty interaction is far more limited than usually occurs in seminar-based instruction.

3   Web-based lectures are sometimes called 'podcasts'.

4   The academic literature on inquiry-based learning is extensive. For recent treatment of this subject, see Lee, V. (ed.) (2012) *Inquiry-Guided Learning: New Directions for Teaching and Learning*, (Jossey-Bass). For international views, see Kahn, P. and O'Rourke, K. (2005) 'Understanding Enquiry-Based Learning (EBL)', in *Handbook of Enquiry and Problem-Based Learning: Irish Case Studies and International Perspectives*, edited by Barrett, T., Labhrainn, I., and Fallon, H. (National University of Ireland, Centre for Excellence in Learning and Teaching). For how inquiry-based learning differs from problem-based learning, see Spronken-Smith, R. 'Experiencing the Process of Knowledge Creation: The Nature and Use of Inquiry-Based Learning in Higher Education' (National Centre for Tertiary Teaching Excellence) (Available at http://akoaotearoa.ac.nz/sites/default/files/u14/IBL%20-%20Report%20-%20Appendix%20A%20-%20Review.pdf; accessed 13 January 2013).

5   See Prensky M. (2001) 'Digital Natives, Digital Immigrants, Part 2: Do They Really Think Differently?', *On the Horizon* (NCB University Press), 9(6): 1–6.

▶ 1 The Socratic Method

1   The Socratic Method is also known as Socratic Dialogue, or the Dialectic Method.

2   For a useful overview of the inquiry-based approach, see Crabtree, E. (2003) 'Improving Student Learning Using an Enquiry Based Approach', Extract from 'Education in a Changing Environment', 17–18 September 2003, *Conference Proceedings* (University of Salford).

3   The term 'active learning' has been in vogue since the 1990s. For an overview of active learning techniques, see Bonwell, C. and Eison, J. (1991) *Active Learning: Creating Excitement in the Classroom* (Jossey-Bass).

4   See Tredway, L. (1995) 'Socratic Seminars: Engaging Students in Intellectual Discourse', *Strengthening Student Engagement*, 53(1): 26–9.

5   For an example of how business schools utilize the Socratic Method, see Barnes, L. Christensen, C. and Hansen, A. (1994) *Teaching and the Case Method*, 3rd edn (Harvard Business School Press).

6   For a concise and informative treatment of the Socratic Method, see Paul, R. and Elder, L. (2006) *The Thinker's Guide to The Art of Socratic Questioning* (Foundation for Critical Thinking Press). For a more theoretical assessment, see Saran, R. and

Neisser, B. (eds) (2004) *Enquiring Minds: Socratic Dialogue in Education* (Trentham Books).

7   Jarvis, P. (ed.) (2006) 'The Professionalisation of Teaching', in *Theory and Practice of Teaching*, 2nd edn (Routledge): 237.

8   Socrates was familiar with economic problems, though on a much smaller scale. Greek city states traded amongst themselves – an early form of economic interdependence.

9   Ironically, though the Socratic Method lends itself to democratic discourse, Socrates himself was deeply sceptical of democratic rule.

10 Scholars have identified different categories of the Socratic Method. For example, see Brownhill, B. (2002) 'The Socratic Method', in Jarvis, P. (ed.), *The Theory and Practice of Teaching* (Kogan Page): 70–8.

11 At one level, the Socratic Method is akin to Austrian American economist Joseph Schumpeter's idea of 'creative destruction' for free market economies, wherein the failure of some ventures clears the way for other enterprises to succeed.

12 Bloom, B. et al. (1956) *Taxonomy of Educational Objectives: the Classification of Educational Goals; Handbook I: Cognitive Domain* (Longman).

13 For example, see http://www.mmiweb.org.uk/downloads/bloomimages/bloom_plts. jpg (accessed 3 January 2013) and the 'Task Oriented Question Construction Wheel Based on Bloom's Taxonomy' (2004) St Edward's University Center for Teaching Excellence (Available at http://think.stedwards.edu/cte/sites/webdev1.stedwards. edu.cte/files/docs/BloomPolygon.pdf; accessed 3 January 2013).

14 For a thoughtful essay on students and their expectations regarding technology, see Carlson, S. (October 2005) 'The Net Generation Goes to College', *Chronicle of Higher Education*, 52(7), A34.

15 In the Pew Research Center survey, 87 per cent said that 'digital technologies are creating an easily distracted generation with short attention spans'. See Purcell, K., et al. (2012) 'How Teens Do Research in the Digital World', Pew Internet & American Life Project (Available at http://pewinternet.org/Reports/2012/Student-Research/ Summary-of-Findings.aspx; accessed 2 January 2013).

16 See Wallis, C. (2006) 'The Multitasking Generation', *Time Magazine* (Available at http://www.balcells.com/blog/images/articles/entry558_2465_multitasking.pdf; accessed 13 January 2013).

17 For example, see Weinstein, R (2004) *Reaching Higher: The Power of Expectations in Schooling* (Harvard University Press).

▶ 2 Prepare your seminar for success

1   For a useful summary of learning environments and their characteristics, see Macdonald, J. (2008) *Blended Learning and Online Tutoring: Planning Learner Support and Activity Design*, especially ch. 4, 2nd edn (Gower): 41.

▶ 3 Introductions and ground rules

1   We adapt the term 'classroom authority gradient' from the concept of the 'transcockpit authority gradient', which describes a potentially hazardous form of interaction (or lack of) between pilots possessing significantly different levels of rank.

The pilot of lower rank normally defers to the judgment of the senior … even when those judgments are in error. See Alkov, R., *et al.* (1992) 'The Effects of Trans-Cockpit Authority Gradient on Navy/Marine Helicopter Mishaps', *Aviation, Space, and Environmental Medicine*, 63 (8), 659–661; see also Hersman, D. (2011) *Safety Recommendation* (National Transportation Safety Board, Washington, DC), 18 May: 3–4.

2   Chapter 10 will address how best to measure outcomes in greater detail. The focus here is the immediate post seminar self-assessment.

▶ 4 Create a positive learning cycle

1   In Europe, these are often referred to as knowledge, skills and competencies, as opposed to knowledge, skills and abilities. For example, see Winterton, J., Le Deist, F. and Stringfellow, E. (2006) *Typology of Knowledge, Skills and Competences* (European Centre for the Development of Vocational Training) (Available at www.cedefop.europa.eu/en/Files/3048_EN.PDF; accessed 8 March 2013)

▶ 5 Encourage discussion and collaborative learning

1   Smith, B. and MacGregor, J. (1992). 'What Is Collaborative Learning?', in *Collaborative Learning: A Sourcebook for Higher Education*, edited by Goodsell, A. *et al.* (National Center on Postsecondary Teaching, Learning, and Assessment at Pennsylvania State University): 11.

2   For the effectiveness of this pairing technique, see Knight, D. (2010) 'Pairing vs Small Groups: A Model for Analytical Collaboration', *Effective Group Work Strategies for the College Classroom* (Magna Publications) (Available at http://blogs. bauer.uh.edu/instructional-design/wp-content/uploads/2010/05/group-work.pdf; accessed 15 December 2012).

3   Scobey, M. (1963) 'Developing and Using Classroom Groups', *Educational Leadership*, 21(3): 152. (Available at http://www.ascd.org/ASCD/pdf/journals/ed_lead/el_196312_scobey.pdf; accessed 15 January 2013).

4   For a detailed treatment of group size and the ability to solve complex problems, see Laughlin, P., Hatch, E., Silver, J. and Boh, L. (2006) 'Groups Perform Better Than the Best Individuals on Letters-to-Numbers Problems: Effects of Group Size', *Journal of Personality and Social Psychology*, 90(4): 644–651 (Available at http://nbu.bg/webs/clubpsy/Materiali%20za%20kachvane/Library/razlichni%20lekcii%20na%20angliiski/When%20Groups%20Perform%20Better%20Than%20Individuals.pdf; accessed 15 January 2013).

5   Rockenbach, B. (2011) 'Archives, Undergraduates, and Inquiry-Based Learning: Case Studies from Yale University Library', *American Archivist*, 74: 278 (Available at http://academiccommons.columbia.edu/catalog/ac:137494: accessed 15 January 2013).

6   Hart, L. (1996) 'Roles: Facilitator, Team Leader, Recorder, Team Members, Process Observer and Others', in *Faultless Facilitations: A Resource Guide*, 2nd edn (HRD Press): 45–60.

7   Tierny, J. (2012). 'What's New? Exuberance for Novelty has Benefits', *New York Times*, 13 February 2012 (Available at http://www.nytimes.com/2012/02/14/science/

novelty-seeking-neophilia-can-be-a-predictor-of-well-being.html; accessed 31 October 2012).

▶ 6 Team teaching challenges

1   Dr. Chris Wickens, an expert in the field of Human Factors, has termed this phenomenon 'Out of the Loop Unfamiliarity', Personal communication with Andrew Bellenkes (1994).

▶ 7 Technology and seminar-based learning

1   Turner, S. (2003) 'Learning in a Digital World: The Role of Technology as a Catalyst for Change' (Available at http://www.neiu.edu/~ncaftori/sandy.doc; accessed 12 January 2013).

2   The University of Melbourne website explains its own LMS (VLE) in detail. Readers who are unfamiliar with LMS may profit from surveying it. (Available at http://www.lms.unimelb.edu.au/start/glance/; accessed 13 January 2012).

3   Adapted from http://cooltoolsforschools.wikispaces.com/Presentation+Tools (accessed 31 October 2012).

4   For a useful overview of such technology, see Martyn, M. (2007) 'Clickers in the Classroom: An Active Learning Approach' *Educause Quarterly*, 2: 71–74 (Available at http://net.educause.edu/ir/library/pdf/eqm0729.pdf; accessed 12 January 2012).

5   Bradley, A. (2010) 'A New Definition of Social Media (Gartner Blog Network) (Available at http://blogs.gartner.com/anthony_bradley/2010/01/07/a-new-definition-of-social-media; accessed 12 January 2012).

▶ 8 Distance learning

1   For a study of how distance learning has been used with students in a Masters of Business Administration (MBA) programme, see Stacey, E. (1999) 'Collaborative Learning in an Online Environment', *Journal of Distance Education/Revue de l'enseignement à distance* (Available at http://web.mit.edu/acs/faq/Online-collaboration/collab-learning_files/stacey.htm; accessed on 12 January 2013).

2   This definition of blended learning is from the Macmillian Dictionary online (Available at http://www.macmillandictionary.com/dictionary/american/blended-learning; accessed January 2013).

3   For a comprehensive treatment of blended learning, see Garrison, D. and Vaughan, N. (2008) *Blended Learning in Higher Education: Framework, Principles, and Guidelines* (Jossey-Bass).

4   For a discussion of how online and face-to-face instruction can complement one another, see Macdonald, J. (2008) *Blended Learning and Online Tutoring: Planning Learner Support and Activity Design*, 2nd edn (Gower): esp. ch. 5.

5   Macdonald (2008): 48.

6   Bersin, J. (2004) *The Blended Learning Book: Best Practices, Proven Methodologies, and Lessons Learned* (Pfeiffer): xviii.

7   Bonk, C., Kim, K.J. and Zeng, T. (2006) 'Future Directions of Blended Learning in Higher Education and Workplace Learning Settings', in Bonk, C. and Graham, C. (eds), *The Handbook of Blended Learning: Global Perspectives Local Designs* (Pfeiffer): 550–67.

▶ 9 End-of-course pitfalls

1   As Dekker notes, 'Complacency is also a name for human error – the failure to recognize the gravity of a situation or to follow procedures or standards of good practice'. Dekker, S. (2006) *The Field Guide to Understanding Human Error* (Ashgate): 120.
2   For an Australian study of how stress impacts academic staff, see Gillespie, N. et al. (2001), 'Occupational Stress in Universities: Staff Perceptions of the Causes, Consequences and Moderators of Stress', in *Work & Stress: An International Journal of Work, Health & Organisations*, 15(1): 53–72.
3   Incident witnessed by Andrew Bellenkes in 1988.

▶ 10 Measure outcomes

1   See Crabtree, E. (2003) 'Improving Student Learning Using an Enquiry Based Approach', Extract from: Education in a Changing Environment 17–18 September 2003, *Conference Proceedings* (University of Salford).
2   Administrators and department heads will be concerned with measures of institutional and programmatic outcomes, respectively.
3   For comprehensive treatment of rubrics, see Stevens, D. and Levi, A. (2005) *Introduction to Rubrics: An Assessment Tool to Save Grading Time, Convey Effective Feedback, and Promote Student Learning* (Stylus Publishing).
4   A racist or sexist remark would constitute a gross infraction meriting immediate instructor intervention.
5   Hampton, M., 'Reflective Writing: A Basic Introduction', University of Portsmouth (Available at http://www.port.ac.uk/departments/studentsupport/ask/resources/handouts/writtenassignments/filetodownload,73259,en.pdf; accessed 12 January 2013). See also Moon, J. (2006) *Learning Journals: A Handbook for Reflective Practice and Professional Development*, 2nd edn (Routledge).
6   For a concise assessment of survey fatigue and how to address it, see Tschepikow, K. (ed.) (2009) 'Rethinking Assessment: Intentional Strategies to Improve Assessment Practice and Protect USG Students from Survey Fatigue', *Student Pulse* (University of Georgia): 3(2) (Available at http://studentaffairs.uga.edu/assess/pdfs/Student%20Pulse%20Summer%202009%20(FINAL).pdf.; accessed March 2013).

Bibliography

Adams, D. and Hamm, M. (1996) *Cooperative Learning, Critical Thinking and Collaboration Across the Curriculum*, 2nd edn (Charles C. Thomas Publishers).

Alkov, R., *et al.* (1992) The Effects of Trans-Cockpit Authority Gradient on Navy/Marine Helicopter Mishaps', *Aviation, Space, and Environmental Medicine*, 63 (8), 659–61.

Anderson, L., and Krathwohl, D. (eds) (2000) *A Taxonomy for Learning, Teaching and Assessing: A Revision of Bloom's Taxonomy of Educational Objectives*, 2nd edn (Pearson).

Bain K. (2004) *What the Best College Teachers Do* (Harvard University Press).

Banner, J. and Cannon, H. (1999) *The Elements of Teaching* (Yale University Press).

Barkley, E. (2009) *Student Engagement Techniques: A Handbook for College Faculty* (Jossey-Bass).

Barnes, L., Christensen, C. and Hansen, A. (eds) (1994) *Teaching and the Case Method*, 3rd edn (Harvard Business School Press).

Bersin, J. (2004) *The Blended Learning Book: Best Practices, Proven Methodologies, and Lessons Learned* (Pfeiffer).

Black, P. and Wiliam, D. (1998) *Inside the Black Box: Raising Standards Through Classroom Assessment* (King's College).

Bloom, B.. et al.(1956) *Taxonomy of Educational Objectives: The Classification of Educational Goals, By a Committee of College and University Examiners. Handbook 1: Cognitive Domain* (Longman).

Bonk, C. (July 2009) *The World is Open: How Web Technology is Revolutionizing Education* (Jossey-Bass) (Book homepage: http://worldisopen.com/).

Bonk, C., Kim K. and Zeng. T. (2006) 'Future Directions of Blended Learning in Higher Education and Workplace Learning Settings', in C. Bonk and C. Graham (eds), *The Handbook of Blended Learning: Global Perspectives, Local Designs* (Pfeiffer): 550–67.

Bonwell, C. and Eison, J. (1991) *Active Learning: Creating Excitement in the Classroom* (Jossey-Bass).

Bradley, A. (2010) 'A New Definition of Social Media' (Available at http://blogs.gartner.com/anthony_bradley/2010/01/07/a-new-definition-of-social-media; accessed December 2012).

Brownhill, B. (2002) 'The Socratic Method', in P. Jarvis (ed.), *The Theory and Practice of Teaching* (Kogan Page).

Carlson, S. (October 2005) '"The Net Generation Goes to College"', *Chronicle of Higher Education*, 52(7).

Crabtree, E. (2003) 'Improving Student Learning Using an Enquiry Based Approach', Extract from 'Education in a Changing Environment', 17–18 September 2003, *Conference Proceedings* (University of Salford).

Dekker, S. (2006) *The Field Guide to Understanding Human Error* (Ashgate).

Duhaney, D. (2004) 'Blended Learning in Education, Training, and Development', *Performance Improvement*, 43(8): 35–8.

Edelson, D., Gordin, D. and Pea, R. (1999) 'Addressing the Challenges of Inquiry-Based Learning Through Technology and Curriculum Design', *Journal of the Learning Sciences*, 8(3/4): 391–450.

Eisner, E. (2000) 'Benjamin Bloom 1913–99' (Available at http://www.ibe.unesco.org/International/Publications/Thinkers/ThinkersPdf/bloome.pdf; accessed 13 January 2013).

Garrison, R. and Vaughan, N. (2007) *Blended Learning in Higher Education* (Jossey-Bass).

Gillespie, N., *et al.* (2001) 'Occupational Stress in Universities: Staff Perceptions of the Causes, Consequences and Moderators of Stress', *Work & Stress: An International Journal of Work, Health & Organisations*, 15(1): 53–72.

Guskey, T. (ed.) (2012) *Benjamin S. Bloom: Portraits of an Educator*, 2nd edn (Rowman & Littlefield).

Hampton, M. 'Reflective Writing: A Basic Introduction' (University of Portsmouth) (Available at http://www.port.ac.uk/departments/studentsupport/ask/resources/handouts/writtenassignments/filetodownload,73259,en.pdf; accessed 12 January 2013).

Hart, L. (1996) 'Roles: Facilitator, Team Leader, Recorder, Team Members, Process Observer and Others', in *Faultless Facilitations: The New Complete Resource Guide for Team Leaders*, 2nd edn (Human Resource Development Press).

Hersman, D. (2011) *Safety Recommendation* (National Transportation Safety Board, Washington, DC), 18 May: 3–4.

Jarvis, P. (ed.) (2006) ' "The Professionalisation of Teaching" ', in Theory and Practice of Teaching, 2nd edn (Routledge).

Kahn, P. and O'Rourke, K., (2005) ' "Understanding Enquiry-Based Learning (EBL)" ', in T.Barrett, I. Labhrainn and H. Fallon (eds) *Handbook of Enquiry and Problem-Based Learning: Irish Case Studies and International Perspectives* (National University of Ireland, Centre for Excellence in Learning and Teaching).

Knight, D. (2010) 'Pairing vs. Small groups: A Model for Analytical Collaboration', *Effective Group Work Strategies for the College Classroom* (Magna Publications) (Available at http://blogs.bauer.uh.edu/instructional-design/wp-content/uploads/2010/05/group-work.pdf; accessed 15 December 2012).

Krathwohl, D. (2002) 'A Revision of Bloom's Taxonomy: An Overview', *Theory into Practice*, 41(4): 212–18.

Laughlin, P., Hatch, E., Silver, J. and Boh, L. (2006) ' "Groups Perform Better Than the Best Individuals on Letters-to-Numbers Problems: Effects of Group Size" ', *Journal of Personality and Social Psychology*, 90(4).

Lee, V. (ed.) (2012) *Inquiry-Guided Learning: New Directions for Teaching and Learning* (Jossey-Bass).

Macdonald, J. (2008) *Blended Learning and Online Tutoring: Planning Learner Support and Activity Design*, 2nd edn (Gower).

Martyn, M. (2007) 'Clickers in the Classroom: An Active Learning Approach', *Educause Quarterly*, 2 (Available at http://net.educause.edu/ir/library/pdf/eqm0729.pdf; accessed 12 January 2012).

Moon, J. (2006) *Learning Journals: A Handbook for Reflective Practice and Professional Development*, 2nd edn (Routledge).

Overbaugh, R. C. and Schultz, Lynn (2012) 'Bloom's Taxonomy' (Available at http://ww2.odu.edu/educ/roverbau/Bloom/blooms_taxonomy.htm; accessed 31 January 2013).

Paul, R. and Elder, L. (2006) *The Thinker's Guide to the Art of Socratic Questioning* (Foundation for Critical Thinking Press).

Prensky, M. (2001) 'Digital Natives, Digital Immigrants Part 2: Do They Really Think Differently', *On the Horizon* (NCB University Press), 9(5): 1–6.

Purcell, K. et al. (2012) 'How Teens Do Research in the Digital World', Pew Internet & American Life Project (Available at http://pewinternet.org/Reports/2012/Student-Research/Summary-of-Findings.aspx; accessed 2 January 2013).

Rockenbach, B. (2011) 'Archives, Undergraduates, and Inquiry-Based Learning: Case studies from Yale University Library', *American Archivist*, 74: 275–289.

Saran, R. and Neisser, B. (eds) (2004) *Enquiring Minds: Socratic Dialogue in Education* (Trentham Books).

Scobey, M. (1963) 'Developing and Using Classroom Groups', *Educational Leadership*, 21(3).

Smith, B. and MacGregor, J. (1992) 'What Is Collaborative Learning?', in *Collaborative Learning: A Sourcebook for Higher Education*, A. Goodsell, R. *et al.* (eds) (National Center on Postsecondary Teaching, Learning, and Assessment at Pennsylvania State University).

Spronken-Smith, R. 'Experiencing the Process of Knowledge Creation: The Nature and Use of Inquiry-Based Learning in Higher Education' (National Centre for Tertiary Teaching Excellence) (Available at http://akoaotearoa.ac.nz/sites/default/files/u14/IBL%20-%20Report%20-%20Appendix%20A%20-%20Review.pdf; accessed 13 January 2013).

Stacey, E. (1999) 'Collaborative Learning in an Online Environment', *Journal of Distance Education/Revue de l'enseignement à distance* (Available at http://web.mit.edu/acs/faq/Online-collaboration/collab-learning_files/stacey.htm; accessed 12 January 2013).

Stevens, D. and Levi, A. (2012) *Introduction to Rubrics: An Assessment Tool to Save Grading Time, Convey Effective Feedback, and Promote Student Learning* (Stylus Publishing).

Tierny, J. (2012) 'What's New? Exuberance for Novelty has Benefits', *New York Times*, 13 February 2012 (Available at http://www.nytimes.com/2012/02/14/science/novelty-seeking-neophilia-can-be-a-predictor-of-well-being.html; accessed 31 October 2012).

Tredway, L. (1995) 'Socratic Seminars: Engaging Students in Intellectual Discourse', *Strengthening Student Engagement*, 53(1): 26–9.

Tschepikow, K. (ed.) (Summer 2009) 'Rethinking Assessment: Intentional Strategies to Improve Assessment Practice and Protect USG Students from Survey Fatigue', *Student Pulse* (University of Georgia): 3(2).

Turner, S. (2003) 'Learning in a Digital World: The Role of Technology as a Catalyst for Change' (Available at http://www.neiu.edu/~ncaftori/sandy.doc; accessed 12 January 2013).

Wallis, C. (2006) 'The Multitasking Generation', *Time Magazine* (Available at http://www.balcells.com/blog/images/articles/entry558_2465_multitasking.pdf; accessed 13 January 2013).

Weinstein, R. (2004) *Reaching Higher: The Power of Expectations in Schooling* (Harvard University Press).

Wickens, C. (1994) Personal communication with Andrew Bellenkes.

Winterton, J., Le Deist, F. and Stringfellow, E. (2006) Typology of Knowledge, Skills and Competences (European Centre for the Development of Vocational Training) (Available at www.cedefop.europa.eu/en/Files/3048_EN.PDF; accessed 8 March 2013).

▶ Websites

http://cooltoolsforschools.wikispaces.com/Presentation+Tools

http://www.lms.unimelb.edu.au/start/glance/

http://www.macmillandictionary.com/dictionary/american/blended-learning

Index